Shoelaces Are Hard

SHOELACES ARE HARD

& Other Thoughtful Scribbles

MIKE McCARDELL

HARBOUR PUBLISHING

Harbour Publishing Co. Ltd.
P.O. Box 219, Madeira Park, BC, VON 2H0
www.harbourpublishing.com

Cover photograph by Nick Didlick
Edited by Caroline Skelton
Cover design by Anna Comfort O'Keeffe
Text design by Brianna Cerkiewicz
Printed and bound in Canada
Printed on 100% recycled paper

Harbour Publishing acknowledges the support of the Canada Council for the Arts, which last year invested $153 million to bring the arts to Canadians throughout the country. We also gratefully acknowledge financial support from the Government of Canada and from the Province of British Columbia through the BC Arts Council and the Book Publishing Tax Credit.

Library and Archives Canada Cataloguing in Publication

McCardell, Mike, author
    Shoelaces are hard & other thoughtful scribbles / Mike McCardell.

Issued in print and electronic formats.
ISBN 978-1-55017-848-7 (hardcover).--ISBN 978-1-55017-849-4 (HTML)

    1. McCardell, Mike. 2. British Columbia--Anecdotes. 3. British Columbia--Humor. I. Title. II. Title: Shoelaces are hard and other thoughtful scribbles.

FC3847.36.M468 2018   C818'.602   C2018-905380-1
                                                  C2018-905578-2

For Ruby and Zoe.
After shoelaces, nothing can stop you.
Now go and do everything.

Contents

Introduction

I started this book with one short, very short, scribbling of a few words. It was about a granddaughter of mine, Zoe. She was having trouble tying her shoelaces. This is something we all go through, and most of us survive.

Shoelaces are about everything in life. Hardship and then overcoming hardship—usually with some help. That help, and overcoming hardship together, make the beautiful poem of being alive.

I wrote a few more short scribbles. The publishers at Harbour said rightly, "No one buys poetry." Not even theirs. I said this is not poetry. These are scribbles. Poems were big a hundred years ago. Now a bit of writing is called a tweet. But I'd rather scribble.

The publishers asked if I would write a book in the regular way: full sentences, no poems. And they, again, are right, so this I have done, sort of. I have slipped in a few scribbles. I hope the publishers don't notice. They are not poems. They are scribbles.

And while I was writing the other full sentences, with commas and periods and that important stuff, I kept thinking of the working title.

Shoelaces Are Hard.

I hope the publishers let me keep it.

Mike

ps… They went for it.

Shoelaces Are Hard

Like All Things Until You Get It

I have to tie my shoes.
Impossible!
When the lace in one hand
meets the lace in the other hand
the lace in the first hand slips off
the lace in the second hand.
Terrible.
"You *can* do it," my big sister said.
But she is big, so she can do it.
I would rather learn to fly.
That would be easy.
But tie a lace? Not so easy peasy.
My sister said,
"If you were on an island with no Velcro,
you would have to tie your laces,
or the tide would come in
and your shoes would float away."
I would rather bake a chocolate cake.
That would be easy.
Except I can't turn on the oven.
Wait! Look! My laces went together!
That was easy.
Now I'll show some little kid,
who needs to tie some laces
how easy it is to get the lace

in one hand around the lace
in the other hand.
Easy peasy.

Empty Toboggan

When You Discover a New Way, It Becomes Your Way

It was the most beautiful sight ever, followed by the most beautiful insight.

We stopped when we saw a small, plastic toboggan coming down the little hill with no one sitting in it. Poor kid, we thought. He had pulled it up to the top and it had slipped out of his hand.

Then, in a classic second later, we saw the kid running down the hill.

Poor kid, but wonderful for us! You cannot get a better story than disappointment overcome by effort and determination and then success. In simple talk, that means a kid running after his sleigh.

We get out. Cameraman Steve Murray gets his camera and I trot up the hill to the two women with the two kids.

"Excuse me," etc., from us.

The gracious, happy woman in charge of the determined boy's world talks to us but the four-year-old has a well-taught view of responding to strangers: He says nothing.

"Shy," says the woman, who is the grandmother.

"Did the toboggan slip away?" I ask.

"No, it's his game," she says.

I am more than happy. Anyone doing anything that is created by themselves is better than things that happen by accident.

The boy does it again. Without warning, of course—what four-year-old lets you know what is going to happen next? He lets go of his ride and chases after it.

Steve, who does not have children and does not know that a four-year-old is not going to wait for him to lift up his camera, grabs said heavy instrument and starts running down the hill taking video of the boy running down the hill chasing his empty toboggan.

And I, knowing this boy will need questioning, chase after Steve who is chasing after the boy who is chasing after the long piece of red plastic.

My arm is still in a sling from me falling off a ladder (that story is still to come), but I have on my snow boots which will hopefully keep me from breaking my other shoulder.

We are flying. Boy who is four, cameraman who is forty-eight and reporter who is seventy-four. Everything is wrong with this picture, but on the other hand this is one of those life adventures that is better than yoga or stress training.

Unknown to me, the boy's grandmother is running behind us.

At the bottom the toboggan stops, boy falls into it and grandmother says, "It's a dream come true for him. It's physics, but he doesn't know it."

I also have no idea what she means, but I've been doing this long enough to know a good quote when I hear it. You have listened to politicians enough to know what they say often has nothing to do with anything, but it *sounds* deep. I think what the grandmother has said actually *is* deep.

We watch Boy go down two more times. It is most beautiful.

Steve gets the pictures of the toboggan going by and the boy's feet going by, which is funny when you put the two together, though it is hard to get those pictures. You have to put the camera on the ground, in the snow, but not get it wet because then it will not work and the engineers will say, "What the heck did you do to this camera?"

And you will say, "I put it in the snow."

And the engineers, who can fix anything but have never been outside and don't know what snow is or why anyone in their right mind would put a multi-thousand-dollar piece of delicate electronics in whatever *snow* is and expect it to work afterwards, say, "We'll try to fix it."

But before the camera goes blank there are pictures of the toboggan and the feet and we are praying the moisture does not seep in before we get one more interview.

"Are you an Olympic skier, or tobogganer?" I ask the grandmother. I am reaching for the impossible. I do this every day. I ask people I have never met if they'll share the greatest story of their life with me.

Sometimes it works.

"No," she says. "But in the south of France where I grew up we had a giant mountain that we tobogganed down."

Oh heavens! To the story god, thank you.

"But when I went back as a grown-up I saw it was no bigger than this," she says, gesturing to the hill we are on, which is about one storey high.

"But we thought it was the biggest."

Oh, Lord. That is life. That is everything. When you are small, your world is big. When you are big, you are shocked by how small your world used to be. And then you look around at your current world and say, "This is big, especially the problems in it."

Too bad we don't get the chance to look back a second time.

This is how the world, and life, changes. Whatever you see now is true. When you see the same thing in ten or thirty years the truth will have changed. It will still be true, but a different true. There is a lesson in that: We should not be so adamant about what we think is true now, ever.

And then four-year-old pulls toboggan up the hill again and climbs on it with grandmother and we hear him screaming screams of delight as they go down the giant mountain.

Did he learn something? You bet. He might not have understood the physics, but he experienced it. And he knew without saying it: It is good to chase a dream, but even better to share it.

Only he didn't see it that way. That is a grown-up way of seeing it. He saw it his way. It was fun.

Frosty the Jailbird

You Are Who You Want to Be, if You Want to Be Who You Want to Be

I t was cold in Burnaby Village, the open-air museum where you learn things that can't be taught in school.

You learn that if you misbehaved in the one-room schoolhouse the teacher would tell you to stand against the wall: nose and toes.

"That's right, young fellow. Put your nose and toes against the wall. I'll tell you when you can stop."

The wall was cold. It made your nose cold. This was why you should not misbehave.

There were four rows of desks and chairs, all bolted to the floor. First row was for first and second grade. The desks were small.

Second row, third and fourth grade. Slightly larger desks.

Third row, slightly larger desks: fifth and sixth grade.

Fourth row, seventh and eighth grade. Those seats were mostly empty.

"Parents needed their kids to work at home more than learn things in school," the teacher said.

The teacher was actually a volunteer who acted the part of the teacher. She was good.

"First thing: inspect their hands. If fingernails were dirty they had to go outside and scrub them," she said.

"Most were dirty," she added. "They had work to do before coming here."

Some of the visiting kids standing around the desks were curling up their hands. They had never heard a teacher like this.

Twenty-five kids in all, maybe more, were in the school in 1920.

"Give lessons to one row, then move to the next and tell the first to keep working."

You can't do that without discipline.

"If someone was really bad I would keep them in after school. That was the worst you could do," she said, "because they had chores at home. Getting wood, cleaning up after the animals."

This was not like the after-school computer games that the visiting kids knew about.

"They were not make-work projects," the teacher said. "They were part of the family's life, and if someone missed doing their jobs someone else had to do them. If I kept them in they would get punished again when they got home."

Then she added, "They were mostly good."

My granddaughters and I went to the General Store.

"That's a bake-it-yourself stove," said the woman behind the counter. "You put the burning wood in this side and the little bit of dough on the other."

I could see two little girls who had never been allowed to light a match—actually I did not know if they knew what a match *was*—pondering this.

"Back then they had a different view of safety," said the woman.

Then outside, Frosty the Snowman was dancing. The song came from a speaker in a tree. Frosty was dancing below it. He was big. The music was happy. Then: "Hi, Mike."

It came from Frosty's non-moving mouth, but I knew the voice.

It was the voice of the street. The voice of the back alley. It was from behind bars. It was from AA meetings. It was from quiet talks between two people, one terrified and lost who was Frosty when he did not have the costume.

"Hi," again.

"Randy, hello," I said to Frosty.

"That's my friend," I said to Ruby, the thirteen-year-old granddaughter.

"You know Frosty?!"

"Good friends," I said.

I had done several stories about Randy on television and written about him in a book.

He woke up one wet and cold morning in an alley just off Main Street. He had no shirt. He was bleeding from his arms and stomach. His head was pounding. He was lost. Broken bottles were on the ground. He could not get up on his knees, much less stand. Another typical morning.

But in one way not typical.

"I said, I either change this or die."

He said those words to me. He told many those same words. He changed. It was hard, harder than you can believe. Some of you who have been there can—but for the rest, no you can't. You have no idea.

Sobriety. No chemicals, no fights, no desperation, no lying, no stealing, no jabbing a needle between your toes because there is nowhere else the skin can take it, no shivering so bad you can't hold the syringe, no looking up to see if someone is going to pull the hypo out of your hand and use it on himself, no screams at the brick wall that does not hear you.

No, now sobriety, which brings a clearer mind which brings a wish, a desire, a darn-it-to-heck need to help others. Randy went on to counselling, helping, talking to—call it whatever you want—others who were in that alley, or other alleys. He changed his world.

He went back to carving and jewellery making and made his pieces well and they were beautiful. And he went on to become Frosty.

We had pictures taken, just Ruby and I. Zoe, the eight-year-old, was still learning about kids who used real fire to bake real bread.

After the pictures I said to Ruby that Frosty was once in prison.

Here was the education: Picture the innocent face, picture the words. Picture the eyes open in disbelief, mouth repeating in total incredulity: "Frosty was in *prison*?"

"And then he became a good guy."

The words ended but the face did not change. *Frosty was in prison?* was one of those lessons you learn but don't know what to do with the learning.

Somewhere between the world of a thirteen-year-old and Randy Tait is Frosty. Frosty the Snowman, who fought through the claws of addiction and crime, and became a jolly happy soul.

It is an advanced-degree lesson in life.

Sometime in the future it will come in handy to my granddaughter, like when she needs to prove to some kids that living is possible even when it seems impossible.

And she learned it from a snowman with a warm heart.

A Child Is Born

The Old Christmas Singalong

It's song time, and you know it.

Handel's *Messiah*. You hear it at Christmas, every Christmas. It is even better than "The Little Drummer Boy" and "Jingle Bells."

It's the one where the orchestra powers up and the choir sings "Hallelujah! Hallelujah!" and you wait for the next "Hallelujah." And there it is bigger and louder and you feel wonderful.

"Unto us a Child is born."

You know, right? You've heard that line. Yes? No?

If you haven't, please look up Handel's *Messiah* on your computer and listen. Do it right now. Put down this book and listen. Please. It will give you something better than Christmas commercials showing people warm and snuggly after they have gotten a loan from the finance company to pay for the presents that another commercial convinced them to buy.

I'll wait.

There. You see what I mean. Even better than "Snoopy vs. the Red Baron."

"Unto us a Child is born."

Beautiful. And the next line.

"Unto us a Son is given."

Wait a minute, she's a girl.

And wait again, she is not given to us. She is Lei's daughter. Lei Wang is the chief security guard at CTV. His usual post is by the elevators where employees get off.

He and his wife, Maggie, were having a baby. Of course his wife was having it and doing all the work and suffering, but it is trendy now to say "we" are having a baby.

Lei did not say that. He gave her all the credit. And he knew it was going to be painful and he worried about his wife's pain. If it was possible to lessen it by increasing his worry he would have crumpled to the ground. He worried a lot. He is a good guy.

Generally men have been useless in this enterprise ever since Adam went off to eat apples while Eve was having a couple of sons. They, by the way, were the first dysfunctional family.

If you did not know, it was one of the sons that killed the other, making Adam and Eve's kids the subjects of the first crime story in the world. But now, back to the delivery room where men are part of the team.

"Team?! What team?" shouts the woman. "I'm working. I'm yelling. I'm screaming. And all you are doing is saying 'push.'"

True, he is not pushing. But he is saying it with gusto.

"Push!"

"I'll push you. And don't you ever—" and this is where she yells, groans, has a look of unbearable pain on her face, then adds, "—don't you ever touch me again!"

And then suddenly there is the naked, wrinkled, slimy creature, the most beautiful being on earth and all is peace and love.

And the next line of the song is "And his name shall be called Wonderful, Counsellor."

Lei and Maggie named their daughter Valerie and Lei continued to worry: Is she breathing? Is she eating? Is she moving? Is she growing? Is she going to have a good life? Will he be a good father?

"Yes, yes, yes, yes. The last two are up to you," we told him.

The "we" are Jasmine Khalil, the receptionist at CTV who sits at a desk next to Lei and who has two teenage sons, and me, who just got off the elevator and has two granddaughters.

We know a thing or two about kids.

"I bought twenty-four diapers. Is that enough?" That was Lei asking.

"Enough for what?" Jas asked.

"For Valerie," Lei said.

"For how long?" Jas asked.

"For how long ..." Lei pondered the question. "How long will she need them?"

He is a first-time dad.

"That might last a few days, if you're lucky," said Jas.

First-time fathers have a brain-numbing learning curve ahead of them.

Every day there was a new picture of Valerie, and every day a new worry.

"Is she too fat?"

"No," said Jas. "She's just right."

Next day, "Is she too skinny?"

"No, just right."

"Is she—"

"Wait, Stop! She is wonderful, beautiful."

If you listened to Handel's *Messiah*, you know the line.

But I didn't say, "Wait, Stop!" I was just thinking, "Please stop asking. Everything will be fine."

Downstairs at the front door of CTV is Yash Bharti, also a security guard and the first line of defence against people who don't like something someone said on the air the previous night or maybe it was another night and they think they heard it but are not sure they heard it right but if they heard it right they want to speak to someone about what they think they heard.

Along with being a guard, Yash is a diplomat. He also has three daughters, so he is wiser than most men. He tells Lei everything will be just fine.

Lei still worries.

I suspect Joseph worried, too, after Mary had a child: "Is he too skinny? Is it okay for him to sleep on his back? What will people think of someone born in a barn? Will I be a good dad?"

The second part of Handel's *Messiah* ends with, "And he shall reign for ever and ever, King of Kings and Lord of Lords. For ever and ever. Amen."

It is so powerful you don't have to believe in anything to be moved into believing in almost everything.

And Valerie's parents, both born in China, both now Canadians, have a child who is now the princess in their lives for ever and ever.

And if you have a child, or children, or grandchildren, or you once had them, or you know someone who has them, and it is Christmas, something special is going to happen.

Yash, by the front door of CTV, who is not Christian, has pictures of his daughters around a Christmas tree.

And Jas, sitting near Lei, who is not Christian, has pictures of her sons around a Christmas tree.

And Lei, who came from a place where Christmas trees were not allowed, is now showing pictures of Valerie and her first little tree.

That is because Christmas is about the birth of a child. And no matter where you're from, what you believe or what language you speak, a birth is a promise of new beginnings. Handel knew that when he composed *Messiah*. Lei and Maggie learned it when their child was born.

Look at the face of some child, any child, and say quietly in your mind to them, "Merry Christmas."

And then listen at least to the "Hallelujah Chorus" from Handel's *Messiah*. And put the two together. Merry Christmas to you.

The Clothesline

The Way You Show Yourself to the World Is the Way It Can Misunderstand You

It's raining when you drive by Linda's house.

"Poor woman, her clothes are all on the line."

It's snowing when you drive by Linda's house.

"Poor woman, her clothes are on the … Wait a minute. Her clothes are *always* on that line."

(Actual comments from those who have ever driven by Linda's house, at least the first few times.)

Linda is an oddball. She is married to Lou, who is an oddball. And there are no two oddballs more lovable than Linda and Lou.

They live in Burkeville and if you have read a couple of my earlier books you know where that is. And if you don't know, it is time you learned because there is almost no more oddball place anywhere.

It has no stores. It has no traffic lights, no sidewalks, no billboards, no bus stops, no restaurants, no cafes, no craft beer parlours, no coffee shops. And it has no peace.

It is at the end of the south runway at the Vancouver International Airport, hence no peace. It was built during World War II for people who were building airplanes in hangars at the other end of the runway. There was no guaranteed way for workers to get to work so Boeing built the homes. Walk to work and walk home, and stuff cotton in your ears when you have breakfast, lunch and dinner, and when you sleep.

"Noise? What noise?" says everyone who lives there as airplanes take off over their heads.

People can get used to almost anything. When my mother found us an apartment in New York City after leaving my father, it was right next to a commuter train line. The trains were non-stop.

On the night we moved in, one of my uncles who was helping us heard and watched the loud blurs roar by.

"How are you ever going to sleep?" I remember him asking.

I slept that night and every night for ten years. Noise? What noise?

Burkeville is like that. By the way, it was named after the president of Boeing at the time. Nothing flies higher than airplanes except egos.

One more thing about Burkeville. It does have clotheslines. Although in the countless times I've been there I have only seen one that is in use, always.

You should go and visit. Walk in a community where everyone walks on the road. Pass people not carrying Starbucks cups. Look at houses of seven hundred square feet which families of four or six said were wonderful.

And then pass Linda's clothesline and hear folks say:

"Hey, that's the way it used to be when I was little. Everyone did it. I helped put out the clothes. That was fun. That's odd to see now."

If Linda comes out, which she might to look at Lou's newest gift to her from a garage sale—their yard is full of Lou's gifts, gnomes, pots, stuff—ask her about her clothesline.

"If I want to wear something it is always fresh. If it's raining, I wear something else."

So simple an answer.

Stop for a minute. That's all. One minute. And look at Linda's clothes on the line. And remember when you watched them fly in the wind and you pretended they were ... whatever you pretended.

The Secret of Tai Chi

Study for a Lifetime, Learn in a Moment

H e was 105 years old.
Date of Birth: March 7, 1913. You would think he would know a thing or two.

Raymond Chung is a master of tai chi. On this, his birthday, he is giving a class in that ancient, mysterious exercise that keeps its practitioners in balance with life.

That is what those who spend their lifetimes doing tai chi say and believe.

Master Chung is in a wheelchair, of course. He slowed down at 102. But his arms and hands are still making the classic push and pull patterns. His voice is gravelly, but you can still make out the words, "Push, pull. Push, pull."

His other words are less clear.

Around him in a semicircle were a dozen residents of the nursing home. All were in wheelchairs, but a few tried to follow his movements. Most were just staring.

Most were in their eighties and nineties. Most where white and had lived their whole lives in a world that was mostly white. Most had never seen someone pushing and pulling except while pushing or pulling a saw, or a baby carriage.

Most had never heard of tai chi, or yoga. Few had ever gone running except to catch a bus. And even in the world they knew, few had ever seen exercise equipment in a gym other than dumbbells and a punching bag.

The world has changed a lot. The idea of working out on a five-thousand-dollar machine that trains your biceps, your triceps and your calves, while also giving you a video readout of how many calories you are burning per minute, was as foreign to them as a watch that keeps track of your heartbeat.

So they stared.

The few who were trying to do the pushes and pulls looked intense. They were finding something new, and that is as exciting when you are ninety as when you are nine. They were also told this was something that would keep them healthy. You can't beat that.

But the simple truth is that everyone in that room was still alive, which is a good way to attend a tai chi class. Of course, the teacher was a good deal older than all of them, which is why everyone was there. But beyond that, the truth is they were all still alive even without tai chi.

Some had smoked for decades. Some had eaten bacon and eggs every day for half a century, or longer. Some had watched a lot of television.

And some had taken vitamins and before they could not walk they had walked. Some had had childhoods where they walked a great deal. Some had not.

What I have seen is some people who take vitamins die young. Some live long. Some who watch their diets gain weight. Some who eat everything stay slim.

What I have noticed is one universal thing. This is the big-ticket item. This is what you and I have been waiting for.

What is the secret?

Master Raymond Chung said—right in the middle of pushing and pulling—he said, "Have good thoughts."

He said, "That is what you need. Good thoughts."

Well, gee. I knew that. And you did too. The secret is so simple. And so very, very true. I have never met a person fat or skinny, tai chi student or couch potato, who has good thoughts and is suffering.

I have never met a person of those categories, who has bad thoughts, who is not suffering.

Tai chi is good exercise. So is throwing a rubber ball against a wall. Before my shoulder was destroyed when I fell off a ladder (don't ask me about it because I am embarrassed), which I'll get to in a later chapter, throwing a rubber ball against a wall was my favourite and basically only sport. After nearly seventy years of throwing a ball against a wall I got pretty good. I could hit the wall. And on the way back I could usually catch the ball. But there is always room for improvement.

Back to tai chi. There is no doubt, no matter what I say, that exercise, moving your body, is good for you. And moving it every day is the one trick to making it work.

I've watched the ladies, and occasionally men, doing tai chi in Queen Elizabeth Park for almost half a century. I've put them on television. They are beautiful. I've watched them in vest-pocket parks around the city. Same thing. Beautiful.

There is usually a master leading the group. He, almost always a he, watches just as Master Chung did in the nursing home. The master sees someone not holding their hand in the exact correct position. It is angled slightly down when it should be angled slightly up, when the left foot is here, not there. But when the left foot is there, not here, the hand should be slightly down, before the foot is here, not there. Then it should be slightly up.

You got that, right?

And then you will feel the chi, which is the power.

What I think, in my Western mind, is that the student never gets it right. So the student comes back the next day to try again. And the day after that. And the day after that.

And it works. It's not the magic, it's the moving every day.

Add some good thoughts and it's worth passing on for another thousand years.

PS

Please don't ask what kind of good thoughts should you have.

You know that thought you have that is bad, the one about someone you don't like? Forgetaboutit. Try thinking something good about someone, anyone. Your blood pressure will go down and you won't have to know any tai chi. You might even live to 105.

Smiles

A Happy Thought Come to Life

I was riding the 210 bus. A lot of people were riding the 210 bus. Almost everyone had a sombre face.

Wait just a moment. "Sombre face" is the fancy way, the academic way, the totally boring and untrue and unreal way of saying it. What does "sombre face" mean?

"Sombre" is blah. It is staring at the ceiling without seeing what colour it is. "Sombre" is dot, dot, dot … Nothing, the face of just sitting and staring and seeing things go by outside the bus as a blur without knowing, caring or thinking what they are, like many on the bus, including me.

Some, many, were staring at their iPhones, of course. Not me. I'm too good for that. I was deep into nothing.

Then I saw across the aisle the six-, or maybe nine- or ten-month-old bundle in her mother's lap. She had a round face and I looked, and she looked, and we were looking at each other.

And I smiled. I wanted to see what would happen.

Don't get me wrong. It was not just a scientific or social test. She was cute, so I smiled.

And she smiled back. Alright, it took a few seconds, but that was all. I smiled and she smiled. She was across the aisle, one row up. She was by the window and I was by the window on the other side of the bus. Far apart. She was less than a year old; I am older.

I could not believe how happy that made me. I made a baby smile. And the baby made me do more of the same.

Her mother looked down at her daughter and then back at me and smiled. That was all. Mother was happy that her child was happy.

I was happy. The girl was happy. I know she was a girl because I saw some pink in the edge of the blanket around her and I live in a world of traditions.

There was nothing else. For one brief moment we had what everyone hopes and dreams of: joy.

I did not want to overdo it. I did not want the mother to think I was a nutcase so I looked away. I looked through the window at the traffic. Then I went back to the baby.

She was looking at me. She was no longer smiling, just looking at me. I was ignoring her. Do we know everything when we are six months old?

I smiled again. I even raised my eyebrows a few times. She smiled a big, toothless, happy grin, almost like she wanted to laugh but not quite.

Talk about magic. Go to magic shows and watch cards disappear or reappear. That's nothing. The girl smiling was magic.

I looked away again and when I looked back she was drinking from a bottle. That was more exciting than the old man on the other side of the bus.

But the old man on the other side of the bus was smiling more than ever.

More on That:

Babies smile when they see you smile.
And that is magic.
Old folks in nursing homes smile when they see you smile.
And that is magic.
You can get a job with one. Or a friend. Or the love of your life.
Without it you are alone. Plus you just feel bad, all the time.
A smile lowers blood pressure,
Or so they say.
It relieves pain. It helps digestion, they say.
It is the great magical medicine.
Smile. Just smile, even in secret.
And the secret of a smile is to first smile with your eyes.
Then you really mean it.

Meditation with a Tree, or a Puck

Looking Strange Is Not Strange if You Believe It

The meaning of life is everywhere. Don't argue. It's true—unless you don't want it to be.

Go into the backyard or a park and find a little flower called a snowdrop which has figured out in its tiny snowdrop brain that if it sleeps under a tree or a bush when it is cold and dark it will be less cold and dark, or at least less cold.

Then it can be the first to push through the dirt and come up into the sun, before it gets crowded out by other plants wanting to do the same thing. That's pretty smart.

What does it mean? Snowdrops figured out how to live without life coaches and personal trainers.

Near some snowdrops is a fellow walking around a tree. He is crouching. He is staring at the tree. He has one hand out with his palm facing the bark. The cameraman starts taking pictures.

I want to talk to this man more than I want to breathe, almost. Come on, how many times have you seen someone walking around a tree and then, wait, he stops, turns and walks the other way? How many times? Me, none.

Walking the other way is twice as good. I wait and wait and do some more waiting. He ignores me. I move closer. I don't want to disturb him but I do want to talk. This is one of those balance-of-life things.

What I see is spiritual, and odd, and ethereal and odd and mystical and odd, and yes, I see a fellow walking around a tree, which is odd.

He must have been doing this a lot because he has worn a circle in the grass, right near the snowdrops.

In an age of combat yoga and hot yoga and fast yoga and intense yoga, a guy walking around a tree is a relief.

He ignores me.

I get closer and hear, coming from one of those trendy portable speakers that don't need to plug into anything, a voice saying, "You are one with the tree. You are the tree and the tree is you."

I am almost next to him and he ignores me. The tree is doing the same thing.

Okay, I give up. I am not going to break his concentration. That would not be right. I start to walk away.

"Wait," he says. "You would like to know what I am doing?"

"Yes, of course, yes and yes." I don't want to seem too excited. But yes.

"I cannot tell you without permission from my teacher," he said.

"Oh," I say, but I think, "you're kidding, aren't you?"

He says he is with a Walking-Around-A-Tree yoga group—with a name I cannot hear, pronounce or picture—and that I can call them and purchase their course and a portable speaker. But that is all he could say.

"Does it make you feel better?" I asked.

"Health. It is about health."

He sees the cameraman and adds, "You cannot take a picture of me without the permission of my teacher."

Well, yes, we can. He is in a public place. On the other hand, I will not use a picture if someone does not want me to. (That, of course, does not count with bad people or politicians.)

But I have failed. I have seen a person walking around a tree and I cannot do a story about him because I do not understand him.

What should be cool is cold. There is no love, fun or insight that I can see. It is probably there, but I can't find it.

I cannot and would not say anything ridiculing or making fun of him because that is wrong. So I won't. But all I see and hear is someone doing something wonderfully odd but following some mysterious rules. It hurts my heart.

Then we look over there. Way over there. A couple hundred steps over there, beyond a chain-link fence. One fellow is skating on inline skates and shooting a ball at a hockey net.

Let's try him.

"How are you?" We talk through the fence.

He stops, he smiles—a big smile, a happy smile. He skates to us. After the hellos he says what he does is not only skate but he "contemplates, radiates and meditates."

That is poetry. It's not *like* poetry. It *is* poetry.

The guy doing the common thing of rollerblading on a concrete hockey rink has the most beautiful yoga-type, or self-improvement-type or holistic-type thing to say while the yoga person has missed the goal entirely.

Robert Quon said he skates here every morning before work, where he fixes bicycles in the back of the A-1 Cycle shop on Main Street. He's been doing this for more than a year and almost every day sees the fellow walking around the tree.

Then he says something which makes me wish I were as good a writer as this skating bicycle mechanic: "This place is a Xanadu of joggers, bloggers, doggers, walkers, strollers and that guy walking around the tree."

"And what do you get from skating?" I ask.

"I radiate."

Oh my gosh. Send me back to writing school and philosophy school and yoga school.

The meaning of life is everywhere. Robert is the snowdrop who figured out that an empty hockey rink is his place to radiate. The fellow walking around the tree who never smiled was doing what someone said he should do. I fully believe he felt good.

I think I saw the meaning of life in both of them. But thank you, Robert.

Stairs

You Don't Have to Pay for What Costs a Lot

S he said she had a new gym membership.

"I can go every night for 150 dollars a year."

Not bad.

"I have weights and a rowing machine and a treadmill and other machines that do everything. And a sauna," she said.

She got a device to wear on her wrist that tracks her heartbeat.

"It has changed my life," she said. "It tells me how many steps I take."

Another woman passed by, healthy, smiling, strong, thin, a bounce in her step.

"What's your secret?" we asked.

"I take the stairs," she said.

A Walk Around the Block

There Is No Training for What Is Best

We did not walk ten thousand steps a day. We did not get our heart rates up. We did not say the word "cardio."

We did not count calories. We did not get sweaty. We did not listen to music through earbuds.

We went for a walk around the block. It was just like in the old days when you would finish dinner and then go for a walk.

We passed a house with a blooming rhododendron. It was orange. We did not talk about Zen, but we were "in the moment" as we passed the bush.

In the winter we passed by this same bush covered with snow. We were "in the moment" then too—to be honest, I don't know what that means, but we were there.

We never checked a watch to see how far we had gone in how many minutes. On the other hand, the passage of time seemed to stop as we walked. It was simply time we spent walking, unmeasured.

We stepped to the side when someone walking a dog came toward us. It is always good to give a little.

Then we said hello, and got a hello and a smile in return, which is not a bad return on such a small investment.

We did not talk about the benefits of aromatherapy. We breathed evening air which always seems to be therapeutic, no matter if you need therapy or not.

Morning air is good also, but who has time to breathe in the morning?

We did not have cellphones. We did not text. We talked, but not too much.

We mostly just put one foot in front of the other, without thought or effort.

It is easier to contemplate feet moving than to try to think of nothing, but I think it has the same result. Quiet. Peace. That is the sort of stuff gurus get paid for.

Never were both feet off the ground at the same time, which was reassuring.

We did not have special shoes, or socks, or tights, or sweatbands, or step counters or goals. And we never felt superior or inferior to those who do.

And one last thing: when we got back to where we started, we felt good, which is not bad.

Walking Is Fun

Getting There While Growing Up

I am five. I fly. I fall. I spin. I walk, two steps then
jump and turn and spin again then race, and win,
And I feel good.
I am ten. Grown-up. I walk straight. I do not jump
like little kids. I walk. Straight.
I am fifteen and walk like my friends walk.
Like this. They walk like this so I walk like this.
I am twenty-five and
"Please, do I have to walk with
the five-year-old?"
She/He does not walk. She/He is a pain.
She/He will never get there.
I am fifty and I walk slowly. I am not in a hurry.
And I don't care if I am late.
I am seventy-five and watch the five-year-olds walking.
I can't dance or spin or fly, or I might fall, and die.
But watching them is being them. And I am five, again.
And I feel good.

Healthy Living or Lunch

I Want a Natural Life, but Why Is Nature Slower than Fast Food?

I t is so hard to be natural. I like ketchup but ketchup is filled with sugar and so it's bad for you, and me.

I want to grow a garden. I want to be healthy. I bought a kit from the dollar store. I will have tomatoes, and cukes and radishes and lettuce and rutabaga. I don't like rutabaga.

I put the seeds in the pots. I watered the pots. Little things grew. In a week I will eat. In two weeks I will eat. In three weeks I will eat.

This is crazy.

I could get a burger in two minutes. I could get a pizza in three.

I forgot to water my pots. Everything died. How can I be natural when nature is slower than pizza?

If nature comes up with a drive-through serving instant cukes in recycled pots that taste like fried meat with a side of fries—organic, of course—I will get natural. So long as there is ketchup on the side.

The Parking Lot Bird

To Be Captured Is Not Always Bad

I t was almost Christmas and we had to get last-minute stuff. You always need stuff. And it is always at the last minute.

We went to Walmart, which we will not tell a close relative who thinks that is a crime.

Do you have someone in your family who developed different consumer values than you?

"You don't shop there, do you? They're not fair to their employees."

That would be our close relative who has honest moral beliefs.

"You don't eat that, do you? It is not humanely treated."

That's someone else telling us what we should eat.

"You don't watch that show? The crew is all male."

That is someone else with strong values.

Yes, yes, and sorry, yes.

So to our close relative, we do not admit we go to Walmart. But we do.

The parking lot is dark and covered with slush and frozen puddles, and cars with tires freezing in the puddles.

My wife and granddaughters run inside to get important last-minute stuff.

My daughter, in the car with me, says, "What's that?"

She points to a bird, a tiny bird, a tiny bird with some colours in its feathers so it is not a normal, natural bird struggling to get out of a puddle and fly to the door handle of a parked car. A normal, natural bird knows better than to get stuck in a frozen parking lot.

This bird flies to the car door handle then slips off and falls, or flutters or whatever birds do, back into the puddle.

"We have to help," daughter says.

Well, yes, we do, but as in all emergencies, unless you are a professional you are not prepared to deal with the emergency.

"The person needs help breathing."

"God, that's awful. What do we do?"

"Breathe into his mouth."

"His mouth? You mean you want me to breathe into his mouth?"

"Yes, or he'll die."

"Do you have a mouth breathing applicator?"

"Why would I have one of those?"

"For an emergency, like this."

"Maybe we can get one at the drug store inside Walmart."

"But we can't go in there. Our son would protest."

It was that way with the bird.

How do you catch a bird in a parking lot in the dark with puddles and ice and headlights passing by? Good question. I had no idea of the answer.

My daughter tries to catch it with her hands. That is like a little leaguer trying to catch a major leaguer's pitch.

"Wow, that was quick."

We corner it. It panics. We get closer. It flutters, flies, shoots out between us.

"We have to catch it or it will die," she says.

She cares. I do too, but this is ridiculous. It may be half-frozen, but it can still move faster than us.

I throw my hat on it. It flies away and my hat lands in a puddle. We close in, but it escapes again.

"Listen, Bird, we are trying to help you," I think. I can't say it because it will scare the bird.

Then someone in the dark says, "Is that you, Colleen?" Colleen is my daughter. The someone is a friend from long ago.

"I saw you two running around the parking lot," he says. "That was kind of strange."

They have not seen each other for twenty years. "Oh, hi, how are you?"

"Good, and you? We're trying to catch this bird."

Friend says let him help. Friend has done fairly well in business. He has an expensive leather jacket with wool around the collar. He takes off his jacket. Snow falls on his shirt.

He stalks the bird, then flings the jacket, that's what he did, he flings his expensive coat over the bird and bingo, coat lands before bird flies. Bird is caught.

Or at least it is pinned under coat on top of puddle in parking lot under falling ice from sky.

"How do we get it out?"

"Well, we could roll up the coat and maybe the bird will stay inside."

That is an option, but coat will then be rolled in slush and salt and tire droppings.

"We could try to reach under it and grab it."

No. We are too smart to think a simple solution would work.

We roll the coat and put it in the back seat of my car and unroll the coat and there is the bird, stunned, standing on the back seat of the car looking like a wet stuffy that will be sent to the garbage. We put an emergency blanket over it.

Coat is dripping. We wring it. It is still dripping. Name of friend: Stanly Laursen. Nice guy. Goes into Walmart with dripping coat.

Daughter follows him and buys bird seed.

Her two daughters come out and try to get into the car.

"Wait! There's a bird in there."

Kids think this is better news than Santa.

"Why didn't you tell us? Why didn't you call us?"

They were stuck in the boring store while real life was outside.

"Can we see it? Can we touch it? Can we do anything on earth to get to something more exciting than last-minute shopping?"

They can't see the bird. It is under a blanket, but still, this is Christmas and birthdays and the last day of school all in one.

Wow!

They get in and we take the blanket off because they might sit on the bird, which is under the blanket, and quickly throw a small towel over it. Why do we carry a towel in the car? Ask my wife.

Stop at the liquor store. No not for the evil, foul, I-wish-I-had-a-sip, ugly, terrible stuff. But for a box.

At home, while the bird's heart pounds in fear below the towel, I cut a square hole in the box, put a screen over the hole and poke some sticks from the backyard into the sides so the bird has places to sit.

Then we put seeds bought at the giant store into the box, and put a dish of water into the box. The water spills. We fill up dish again and put it on top of puddle in box.

Then. How do we get Bird from towel to box?

Uh. Maybe we can put the towel inside the box, then unroll it and take the towel out when the bird is free.

We lower the towel through the top of the box. Daughter is ready to close the top flaps in case the bird tries to escape.

Except my arm pushes the flap more open than she can close and the bird escapes.

And the poor bird does a crazy flight for freedom right into a wall, bounces off, and heads to the curtains. Granddaughters have not seen anything this good since the previous Christmas morning. In fact, this is better.

They scream, which encourages Bird to fly again, this time landing on big old plant in the front window.

If we throw a towel over it we will knock over the plant. That would cause wife to express her displeasure, which is to be avoided.

"Girls, chase the bird away from the plant."

"No. We don't want to scare it."

"Please chase the bird away so we can catch it."

"Can't we just leave it there? It looks happy."

I chase Bird. Kids hate me.

It lands on another plant in another room. The old jade plant that is made of iron.

In 1973 when we moved to Canada my wife went to Woolco, which was where Walmart is now. She came back with a sixty-nine-cent plant in a tiny plastic pot.

I had never had a plant before. I thought plants were in parks and I was not sure what a park was. Actually, I never thought plants were anywhere. In New York plants were unknown, at least to me and everyone I knew. We had concrete.

But now I had a jade plant in a plastic pot. I watered it. It survived. Forty-five years later it is still surviving, in a much, much larger pot. It has had many children from pieces that have broken off, which have been given away. Some of them are still alive.

The bird was now sitting on this jade plant, which I could hit with a shovel and it would not flinch. A dish towel was not going to hurt it.

Wrong. In grabbing the towel after it covered the bird I knocked over the invincible jade plant. It now had one fewer jade arms.

But the bird was in the towel and then we moved it to where it was terrified again inside the box. Having animals in the house is so calming.

Ruby, then thirteen years old, was trying to identify it on her tablet. I have no idea how she or anyone finds things on the internet. I would have gone to the library. Zoe, then seven, was dropping seeds on the bird's head after opening the top of the box after we told her not to open the top of the box.

"It won't escape. I'll be careful."

Then she closed it. How can you get mad at someone trying to feed a starving, lost, bewildered creature?

Ruby learned its name.

"Wow! We have an Australian zebra finch."

We had no idea how it got into the parking lot. It may have escaped from an open window or from someone bringing it home from a pet shop or it may have been dropped by an angel who wanted to see what would happen. Angels do weird things.

A few days later after it had learned to hop from the branch on one side of the box to the branch on the other side we decided that it deserved a better life.

I said we could go to the Bloedel Conservatory in Queen Elizabeth Park, which is filled with birds, and there we could secretly release it.

"No!" I was told by everyone. "It's not right to do something sneaky."

Okay, I have much to learn in life.

I called the conservatory and Agnes Romses, who is in charge of everything there, tells me they cannot take that kind of bird because it is a prolific breeder. If something tragic happens to a mother bird the other birds, even males, will sit on the dead bird's eggs until they hatch.

They once took in seven of these birds, Agnes said. "A year later we had two hundred."

The crew under the giant dome spent weeks with nets catching them and turned them over to a society that raises such birds.

We gave her our bird in a box, which she said she would give to the society. It would have a good life, she said. Then we walked around the conservatory filled with birds over our heads and fish below our feet, and with our refugee guaranteed a life better than an icy parking lot.

"This is more fun than last-minute shopping," said someone, or everyone.

Miracles Are Free

It Does Not Matter Where You Look, You Get What You Want

I think if you just keep open to the possibility that the impossible can happen, in fact, it will happen. There is no trick to it. You just believe it.

I wanted to do a story on the ss *Beaver* for the never-ending Friday history series. I also have to do a second story on the day I do the history lesson, which makes that day very exciting—and impossible. Some days it takes a miracle to get both of them done.

But back to the history.

One hundred and forty years ago the *Beaver* was the most famous ship on the west coast. She was the first steamboat. She was a workhorse, a passenger liner and a boat for all seasons. She was fast and did not need wind in her sails, which she did not have. She got people to places they could not get to without her.

She was odd looking. Sort of like the first cars without horses pulling them.

She had a large paddlewheel on one side which was powered by steam which came from a boiler filled with sea water and was heated with a wood-burning firebox. The boilers had to be replaced every few years, but the ship lasted fifty-three of those trips around the sun. She was said to be indestructible.

She served the Hudson's Bay Company from the mouth of the Columbia River between Washington and Oregon up to Alaska. She worked in the gold rush in the Fraser Canyon. She was used by the British Navy. She was a good ship.

And she was wrecked at Prospect Point, just under where the Lions Gate Bridge was later built.

And I was bored by the story. Yes, the ship was hard-working and reliable and sturdy, and those are good traits. But in a good story something must happen, something odd or ridiculous or wonderful or stupid. Anything.

Someone walked across the street in the crosswalk with the light and got to the other side.

That happens a lot, thank goodness. But you don't run down the street and say, "Someone made it to the other side and nothing happened!"

It is a sad truth. What we as humans crave—besides food and warm, snuggly companionship and new shoes and a raise at work and a decaf double-espresso latte with sprinkles—is something very human.

We want excitement.

Did you see the Lamborghini with an *N* on the back and a dent in the front fender?—if that twenty-thousand-dollar sliver of metal on the two-hundred-thousand-dollar thing built to carry a loud muffler even *is* a fender.

Now that is a story.

Anyway, I had heard about the *Beaver* forty-five years ago when I first started writing about things in BC, and I did not care. It was another ship that had sunk. There were probably a hundred ships that sank around Vancouver Island and up the Inside Passage and near the First Narrows into Burrard Inlet.

It was a rough area. There were rocks to hit and probably mermaids leading sailors to them. Ships sank. The *Beaver* was not an exception.

Then I got interested in beer in Vancouver. That is a subject to keep you happy, even if you don't drink.

I read in a book about the history of beer that there is more beer consumed in the world than water, tea or coffee. I don't know if it is true. People write all sorts of things in books. But I read somewhere else that there is more beer consumed than Coca-Cola, and for that we can be thankful.

Beer is older than wine. All you have to do is throw some weeds into a barrel, add some water and wait. And you don't have to wait very long, not like wine.

In a couple weeks the water starts bubbling and presto, beer, or ale or bitters or whatever you want to call it is ready. It is the drink of the poor, the working class, and the trendy at a new craft beer restaurant that serves two hundred varieties. And it tastes good, if you like it.

In Vancouver in the late nineteenth century there was no other drink. Sure, water was fine, but beyond that there was not much whisky because it had to come from far away. And there was no wine—are you kidding? Can you see a fellow who has been chopping away at trees that were taller than some West End condos asking for a glass of Chardonnay after work?

No. Just beer. And lots of it. At a location that is now Main and Broadway there was a beautiful, powerful, clear and clean creek way down in a deep ravine. It did not dry up in the summer, and that was important, because that is when beer is most wanted.

Around it were built seven breweries and the creek was named, brilliantly, almost as though they had a bright advertising copywriter handy, Brewery Creek. It could have been the Creek That Saved Vancouver, or the Creek With The Flavour Of Racoons Washing Their Paws In it, or something like that, but Brewery Creek became the fountain of happiness for the tiny city.

The breweries worked seven days a week, twenty-four hours a day. They supplied saloons that were open seven days a week, twenty-four hours a day and had customers seven days a week, twenty-four hours a day.

The sawmills would not allow their workers to drink while working. That was not to protect the workers. They were replaceable. It was to keep blood off the freshly cut cedar planks.

But right outside the boundaries of the mills were the saloons. Beer after work, beer before work, so long as there was no beer during work.

Unless you were working on a boat. Then no one would tell you No. And one of those boats was the ss *Beaver*.

I learned this in one line, in one caption, under one picture of the *Beaver* up on the rocks. It said something about the inebriated crew running out of beer and trying to turn the ship around to go back for more when it hit the rocks. I did not know this was common knowledge back then.

In that one line the story of the *Beaver* came to life. It was sad, it was awful when it happened, and I hate when bad things wreck good things, but it is those things that people talk about and remember.

We are a strange species.

So I would do a story about the ss *Beaver*. One place to go was the Vancouver Maritime Museum where they have the anchor.

The cameraman Murray Titus and I go to Prospect Point where the accident occurred. He takes pictures of the water and the rocks and the stone monument remembering the *Beaver* on the land above it. Then we go to the museum.

We drive slowly along Pacific Avenue in case we see something to put on television. Murray starts talking about some friends of his from high school. I am jealous because I remember no friends from high school. He misses the turnoff to the Burrard Bridge.

"Aren't we going to the museum?"

"Of course. I meant to turn but I was talking."

You can't argue with honesty.

We get to the parking lot of the museum at eleven thirty, which is late. I like to be done with the history story as quickly as possible, so we can look for the other story that will air that night.

He parks, I get out, he gets his camera, and at the same moment a small blue car pulls into the parking lot.

Driving is an older man with a white beard and a wonderful, happy face. He is a sailor, I think. Next to him is a woman with a smile and tinges of blue in her hair. She is a rebel.

I see their faces and think that I would love to do a story about them. I think this in a half nanosecond, because it doesn't take long to have a thought.

I also know this is not going to happen because they are looking for a parking spot and they are doing nothing unusual and we are going inside to take a picture and I will never see them again.

"Hi, Mike," says the wonderful face with the white beard.

"Hello," I respond, without stumbling over the word.

They say they saw us and just wanted to say hello.

That's nice.

They say they watch every night.

That's wonderful.

I ask where they are going. They tell a long story about their need for a miracle. You can't get a better story subject than someone who needs a miracle, except someone who gets it.

Her name is Eunice. His name is Al. She has cancer in her eye. She has taken much radiation therapy.

Yesterday her eye began bleeding. They called her specialist at UBC. She was told they have a two-month wait. Then she was told, wait a moment.

"Come tomorrow."

"It was a miracle," she says. "I believe in miracles."

My heart smiles. What you believe, you get. Flat truth. Don't argue.

She talks about being in a bus station in Calgary when a woman tapped her on the shoulder. "Aren't you Eunice?"

Eunice hesitated. She did not know this woman. Cautiously she said yes.

"I'm your sister Becky."

Eunice had not seen Becky for forty years. After their mother died the family split up. Eunice was the youngest and had no contact with her siblings.

"Miracles are a state of mind," she says, "just like joy and happiness and all those things."

How did I not stick my head into the car, across Al who was behind the wheel, and say to Eunice, "Yes! That is what I believe. That's all there is to it."?

The problem with all this wonderful good talk is the car is small and low, and Murray is on one knee pointing his camera in through the open window.

And his knee is killing him. He told me earlier he had put a brace on it that morning because it hurt so badly. But he is holding the camera steady. I have to finish this quickly or he will die, or at least groan.

"And what miracles have you had?" I ask Al.

At that moment I can see through my straining peripheral vision Murray trying to get both knees down then switch knees without moving the camera.

You ask why he did not just say, "Wait a second, wait while I move a bit." But people who take video pictures for television are a different breed than the rest of us. I never met one who stopped shooting for anything, including—hold your stomach for a moment, in fact, skip the rest of this sentence—the one who vomited to the side while on a bouncing float plane and still held the camera to finish recording someone's commentary.

And Murray keeps going and Al says, "My miracle was marrying Eunice on my sixty-fifth birthday."

Then they drive off to get to her doctor appointment. We wish her luck, but she is already expecting a miracle and that is better than luck.

And then we go into the museum to take a picture of the anchor of the *Beaver*.

Trace that back. I try to do it after every story. How did we see or glean or find this wonderful thing that goes from someone way over there doing something to ending on television that night? How in the world did we meet Eunice and Al at just that moment?

If Murray had not missed a turn by talking, there would have been no meeting. One minute's, half a minute's difference on either side and we would not have met.

Call it coincidence, call it dumb luck. It was a miracle. They were our story for the night.

There is no way you are going to even suggest to me miracles don't happen. If you do, Eunice would like to give you some talking to.

Try telling her that getting an appointment with a specialist without waiting two months is anything else.

Honestly, you know better.

We went on to look at the anchor of the *Beaver* and found something else.

Ship of Bones

When You Have Nothing, Anything You Have Is Everything

You want to see something really cool? Really?

And as soon as folks see it they say, "What? Really?"

Then they add, "Cool! Really!" Because what else can you say when you see a model ship that looks like so many of the other models in the Vancouver Maritime Museum, which are intricate and realistic and simply beautiful? And then you learn it is made of bones.

What?

Bones, just like I said.

This story is first a story of the amazing ingenuity of people. Second, it is a story of the miserable cruelty of people. I don't like the second part.

I'll get to it in a second, but first I'll explain how one thing leads to another.

The Vancouver Maritime Museum, the forgotten museum that I think is better than the big-time museums: all ships, all the time. They have the anchor of the ss *Beaver*, the ship sent to the dark deep by a crew of drunks. (That story is just before this story if you are jumping around.)

We photograph the anchor, and then the museum curator, Duncan MacLeod, asks us if we want to see the bone ship.

Well, yes, of course, whatever.

Both the cameraman Murray Titus and I think that if this bone ship is a ship made of bones, it will look like a ship made of bones. That is the trouble with having preconceived thoughts. Avoid them.

We see behind a display case a magnificent model of a sailing ship, all in white, much like many of the others in the museum.

Bones?

All bones.

Duncan explains, as does the caption below the ship, that it was made during the Napoleonic Wars between England and France in the early nineteenth century. The world is always at war. How did Napoleon get in power? How do crazy people get in charge of countries? Sad. And it seems like it never stops happening.

But in this war when sailors from either side were captured they were put in a dungeon and forgotten. It was not like they would be released after the war because wars never end.

No television. No books. No weight-lifting room. So some of them made models of ships, the only things they knew.

Many of the sailors were from the poorest classes. That is why they became sailors who shot cannons. A few survived. Some died. Some had arms and legs amputated on the wooden decks, and some got captured. It was not a good life. But some of them were artists, or they became artists after months or years in a dirty cell with little to eat and nothing to do. They recreated the world that got them there.

They made beautiful copies of ships they had served on.

How do you make a model ship? They didn't have kits. They didn't have balsa wood. They didn't have anything.

Some found scraps of wood. Others did not. The only thing they had were the bones of cows and pigs that the guards stripped of meat and then threw to the prisoners. The prisoners scraped off the minuscule bits of flesh. No, they scraped off the imaginary bits of flesh because there was nothing left.

Then some of them took the bones, after the marrow had been sucked out, and cut tiny planks from the once-living piece of white hardness. How did they do this? They had no tools. Rocks? Fingernails? Yes. But something else.

Tell you in a minute.

They cut slivers from the bones and put them together and made copies of war ships that were accurate to the smallest detail. That sounds like a cliché, but it is true.

The official model builder at the museum, Lucian Ploias, tells us that he put a miniature camera into the ship we were looking at and found the entire interior was reconstructed in detail and scale. No one could see it.

Cool.

Then he tells us that this particular model must have been built by a shipwright because every door handle, every wheel on every cannon and every porthole is the way it should be.

He shows us a poorly made model, which looks fabulous to me. It was also made of bones. It is beautiful.

"It's third rate, at best," says Lucian.

Oh.

But this one, the first one you will look at if you go to the museum, is a work of art, worth a fortune now.

Wow.

Now the bad news.

Lucian says that the models were also worth a lot when the French and English were still blowing up each other's real ships.

So dungeon guards would find prisoners who had talent and give them extra food and better sleeping areas.

And then they would give them tiny knives to carve the bones with. Not knives big enough to escape with, but sharp enough to cut bones, if you had enough time.

And the prisoners had that. They would be there for life, or until their country won the next war and emptied the dungeons. But you had to wait for the war and then you had to wait for the outcome and then you had to wait for the negotiations by people who did not know you were waiting.

"This ship is probably from one of those who was waiting. It's beautiful. The prisoner would have gotten nothing for his work."

That is Lucian again. And that is the part I don't like. The part where the artists got survival, and nothing else, in return for a lifetime of work.

And that is the end of the story.

Go to the museum. Walk on the deck of the *St. Roch*, which chugged across the frozen North Sea at the beginning of World War II to claim the top of Canada for Canada.

The ship was stuck for two years in the ice. It was not nice.

Then look at the wonderful models. Then visit Lucian who is making a scale model of the *St. Roch* that will take him two years.

Then look at the bone ship.

And think of the prisoners with such talent.

The beautiful part of this story will make you say "Wow." The cruelty will make you sad.

The Best Ocean Cruise

Having It All Is Only a Matter of What You Want

Y ou go down a long sloping plank that leads to the water.

There is your ship, waiting. It is a little scary because you have never gone on a voyage before. Did you pack the right things? Will you get sick? Will you meet other passengers? Will you meet the captain?

Lots more questions, but the other passengers are already boarding. In line, inching forward. Excited. Worried. Excited. Okay, worried, because sometimes ships do sink and even if you can swim, the water will be cold and can you save anyone else while trying to save yourself, and will anyone save you and will they come and rescue everyone?

Yes, the questions are jumbled. But this is serious stuff. I—*we*—could die.

I know everyone tells you it never happens. Yeah, sure. Never happens. What about the *Titanic* and other ships you don't know the names of? What about them, huh?

You board. It is steadier than you thought, but still, a swell may come and you have to be careful. Don't let go of whatever you are holding.

And then you are off. The departure was so smooth you did not even notice. You are underway. That's the way they talk on ships: "underway."

You are out now on the ocean, passing the big buildings in the harbour. You, I, have never seen them from this side and they are wonderful. Wow, all those people in those windows looking at our ship. Bet they wish they were down here with us.

We pass other ships and the passengers are waving. That's another seagoing tradition. Waving at people on other ships even though you have no clue who they are and have never seen them before and will never see them again.

Unless some night in a smoky bar … Wait, there are no more smoky bars. Unless some night in a bar with very clean air you meet a stranger and you find out you were sailing on the same day from the same port and you strike up a friendship and get married. And you always joke that you may have waved to each other as your ships passed. Romance is always possible on the sea.

I'll cut this short. I—*we*, because I had my nearly lifelong companion on this voyage—got to see places we have never seen. We talked with the captain who told us secrets behind some of the major yachts we passed. Some of them are only bought to take advantage of tax loopholes. Who would have guessed?

And then we ended our trip. We were thankful, happy, fully refreshed and ready for a stroll across Granville Island.

We said goodbye to our Granville Island ferry and the kind captain and went off to dinner, which cost more than the ride.

Round trip from behind the market down to Science World and back to the market is seven dollars. At least for seniors.

And we did not sink.

The Spotter

A Teenager in Love Is Whenever You Are in Love

He was alone. Grass around his shoes, barbed wire fence in front, standing far off from the end of the runway. But he was not alone. He was in love.

He was alone when his wife died. That was after a long and happy marriage.

Then she died, which broke his heart and left him alone. He was not feeling sorry for himself, he was sad that she was no longer experiencing the life they had together, which was full of joy.

Then time passed. Much time.

But as things happen in the impossible-to-explain universe that gives and takes life and everything else, the husband of a friend also died.

The widow and the widower had been friends thirty years ago.

They met again, accidentally. How does that happen?

"Unbelievable," he said.

Now he stood alone at the end of the runway with binoculars. She was going to Calgary for two days. He wanted to watch the plane take off.

"You are like a teenager in love," I said.

"Yes," he said. And then said, "Yes," again.

He watched the liftoff. A grin from here to there, and back again if that was possible.

He would be seventy-one in a week. And he was no longer alone.

Forklift

The Story That Makes the Next Story True

"No, she should not do it. No, she should not let her kids do that kind of thing. That's silly, borderline dumb, wrong, and someone should *do* something!"

Those were the words from the Granville Island regulars, who consider themselves slightly superior to supermarket shoppers.

I know what they were saying when they passed by the woman with her four-year-old twin boys climbing on a forklift because I heard them. This was worse than shopping in a supermarket. This was plain *wrong*!

"Doesn't she know how to bring up her kids?"

The kids were turning the wheel on the forklift and saying, "Varoom, varoom."

This tiny spot with a parked forklift had become a playground of total imagination. It was not designed by a child psychologist, with a cushioned surface of shredded car tires so no one would get hurt, not this one.

Of course not getting hurt is important. But falling on something hard and crying and getting hugged is also important. And you learn something from that, that you don't learn from shredded, thoroughly cleaned, car tires.

And besides, the kids' mother was watching, and close by and ready to hug.

But I could see condemnation in the frowning, pinched faces of the two women who were watching. Pinched faces because that is the way people look when they don't like the way someone else is doing something they don't like.

"What's happening to motherhood these days?" one of them said, or I think she said that because I could just barely hear. Maybe she said, "That woman should be reported."

I don't know which she said, and I don't know to whom the mother would be reported. Maybe to the Minister of Everything Important To Children, who would give her a warning.

I was thinking, "Isn't she wonderful! Isn't she brave? Isn't she the mother you had, or wished you had, or want to be?"

Varoom, varoom. That is fun.

Let us start at the very beginning, a very good place to start. A cameraman and I drove past the forklift, saw the woman and the kids and I said, "Whoa, stop, now—wow!—quick before it goes away."

I jump out, he stops, in that order. He gets out the camera but I am already talking to Mother, as quickly as I can, leaving out *the*s and *and*s and punctuation because I don't want her to go away or say no, or think we are intruding on her life, which we are, so I talk fast.

"Hate to bother you, it's none of our business, but that is the most wonderful thing I've seen all day."

I always say that because I mean it. If it were not true we would not have stopped.

"This is beautiful," I say.

I mean what I say and for that moment the kids on the forklift are Michelangelo on the ceiling.

Her kids love climbing on it, she says.

"Can we take a picture?" Always the same question, not always the same answer. Sometimes yes, sometimes no, sometimes "my hair doesn't look good, so I have to decline."

That happens more often than you would believe. Although you probably would believe it because you have heard it when you've gotten out your camera.

No. My hair! No. My makeup!

Beauty, reality and life are forgiving. Makeup hides all that. You climbing over that fence or log is beautiful. You don't need makeup.

Back to the woman with her kids on the forklift. It is parked outside the main entrance to the market on Granville Island.

"You think this is okay?" I ask. Because I don't want to get anyone into any kind of trouble even if I believe this trouble is the kind people should get into.

She says she talked to the driver of the forklift, asked if it was okay for her boys to play on it, and he asked, "Do they have a licence?"

So she knows it is okay.

And we take pictures of them. And they are wonderful.

Remember when you climbed on top of a car with your friends? Maybe you never did. We did, in the distant past when not everyone had a car but your friend's friend's father had one and you thought, "Wow, let's climb on it."

We can drive, we really can, or at least we can climb on it, and the roof was strong enough to hold four or five kids—can you see that happening now? Plunk, collapse, dent, trouble. But car roofs were stronger then, and we climbed. And it was exciting, and sixty-five years later I remember riding on the roof of that car that felt like a rocket ship even though the car was in a garage and going nowhere.

And this woman was letting her kids sit in the seat of a forklift that was not lifting.

"I can drive it," said one of the four-year-olds who looked like the other four-year-old.

"Really?" I asked.

"No, not *really!*" he said in the frustration of dealing with someone who was not smart enough to know when things were not real. "I'm only pretending," he said.

That from a four-year-old who is smart enough to separate pretending from reality, unlike some adults.

Remember when your mother, if you are old enough, said, "Go out and play and be safe and come home when the street lights come on"?

The forklift was not that. Those days are over. But this mother was saying, "You have those little trucks at home. This is a real one. Climb on up. I will watch."

Then came the security guard: "That's not a plaything. Get them off there, please."

She did. She felt bad. She worried that she would get someone in trouble. She went into the market.

I followed to tell her she was wonderful and not to worry because she did have permission and no one was hurt and hundreds of thousands of people later that night would say, "Right on. Wish my kids were doing that."

But I could not find her. I went by the fish and the fruit and the crafts. Nothing. She was gone.

I was afraid she would go home and worry.

The story ran on the news. Many said it was exactly the way the world should be.

The next day the chief boss of all bosses passed by me.

"Nice forklift," he said.

Yes, nice forklift. The way kids should play, if you are brave enough to let them.

Six months later I saw the mother with her two sons near a playground.

"That was the best thing ever. Thank you," she said.

She was not worried.

Playgrounds

The Story After That Story

Adam and Eve's kids, at least the ones who did not kill each other (every family has its problems), had fun playing just outside of Eden.

That would be the Garden of Eden, which had the world's best playground. We don't know what that was like. The gates were closed.

But we can guess Adam's remaining kids got some bricks and boards—please don't tell me there were no bricks and boards back then. The kids found them in a back alley—and they made a see-saw and rode up and down until one kid fell off and got hurt.

The other kids said, "That didn't hurt."

That's the way kids say things when they see one kid crying. They don't want him to cry because then his mother will come out and say, "What is going on here?!" And everyone will have to stop playing.

So the other kids say, "That didn't hurt." And that is good enough to make the kid stop crying and get back on the board. And soon it doesn't hurt.

It worked that way through the Old Testament and the New and the Middle Ages and the Renaissance, and right up until about one generation ago.

And then came the 1990s and the 2000s. And the PC people got involved. Those are the Playground Correct people. Those are the ones who were really tempted by the devil to eliminate fun and replace it with worry.

First, eliminate the see-saws. "Kids could get hurt when it hits the ground."

Second, take out the monkey bars. "Kids could get hurt when they hit the ground."

Third was the ground itself. "Kids could get hurt when they hit it."

It became a cushioned ground made of rubber that was softer than a baby's cheek.

Out went the corners of playhouses. "Kids could get hurt if they bumped into them." All corners became curves, nice soft edges which are not real edges and cannot momentarily dent a kid's baby soft cheek. Cheeks, by the way, are made to spring back after being momentarily dented.

And the PC people were happy watching the kids not getting hurt or dented.

And the parents watched and talked to each other and drank their lattes made with fair trade beans and organic milk, and tweeted pictures of their kids standing on the rubber ground and standing on the rubber ground and standing on the … Wait a minute.

The kids aren't playing. They are standing around talking to each other and drinking vitamin-infused water, and some of the older ones are playing video games on their parents' hand-me-down last generation iPhones.

The kids come to a playground and say, "There's nothing to do." And they're right. They get pushed on a safe swing over a rubberized safe ground, or get turned on a safe turning thing which cannot be pushed too fast so that the kids cannot fall off onto the rubberized ground, or they go into a playhouse with a smooth entrance and smooth corners and sit on the rubberized, safe, non-denting ground and say, "This is boring."

Right on, kids.

But now comes the revolution. You may have seen this. It made the *New York Times*' front page so we are talking officially important.

Some people in England are experimenting with a new kind of playground. It has bricks and boards and boxes and sand and sticks.

And the first thing kids do when they go in there is play. They play soldier with the sticks, which is not allowed anywhere else. They play digging with the sand, which is not allowed anywhere else. And they make a see-saw with the bricks and boards and play on it. And when a kid falls and gets hurt the other kids say, "That didn't hurt."

And the kid gets up and plays some more.

Adam and Eve of course are watching all this and saying: "Finally! We have some descendants who are not totally embarrassing."

The Hammer

What Is Really Memorable? Something That Fits in the Memory of Your Hand

I am pounding wooden stakes into the ground. They are as tall as my waist.

I will wrap plastic yellow ribbons from one end to another to make a fence, so that tonight on Halloween kids will not run across flower beds where next year's beauties are sleeping.

The hammer in my hand feels so comfortable, except for two gouges which dig into my thumb.

And I look at the black tape on the neck of the hammer and it looks so out of place.

I got the hammer when I was ten.

Someone, I don't remember who, gave me the hammer and a screwdriver and a pair of pliers so I "would have some tools like a guy should have."

I remember the someone saying that, and then the someone left. I don't remember who the someone was.

I did not know what to do with the tools. I had no nails, I had no screws and I had nothing to squeeze with the pliers.

I had no father, no brothers. This was a fact of life.

But the hammer felt so comfortable in my hand.

I wished I knew how to use it. I tried swinging it in the air. But that is hard to do without hitting yourself. So I put the hammer and the other tools under my bed.

Over time the screwdriver and pliers were borrowed or lost.

A year or so later I picked up the hammer. It felt so good. But I was embarrassed.

I did not want anyone to know I had never used it.

So I took a sharp kitchen knife and dug two gouges in the handle to make it look used. And I took some black tape, the kind I had seen workmen using, and wrapped it around the wood on the neck of the hammer.

Time passed. Life came.

I left home. Got married. Children. Projects. Dollhouse, broken stairs, removing nails, fixing this, fixing the other thing and then working on that other thing. You know, the thing that never gets fixed.

All fixed, or still to be fixed, with the hammer.

Years passed. Decades passed.

The hammer hung on nails at the back of the garage, coming down every week or so to fix this, then that, and crack ice on the driveway in the winter, and bang back nails in the porch in the summer.

And there were lids of paint cans that needed sealing.

And tonight there were stakes that needed pounding into the ground.

There are not many things I have, in fact nothing else, that has grown old with me. I know you have something that you had when you were small and still have. And I know it has some meaning. That makes us both lucky to have them.

More than six decades after that someone gave it to me, the hammer still feels so good.

Except for those stupid grooves from the knife that still rub against my thumb. And no one ever, never, not once did anyone ever say, "Wow, that looks like a well-used hammer. You must be a real fixer-upper."

Never.

Let Me Talk About Me

Two Ears, One Mouth—Let the Poor Thing Rest a Bit

"I went to the store yesterday and—" I was saying to a friend, when …
"I went to the store, too," she said. "And I got the most amazing teapot. It was on sale and it was blue and it was neat and then I went to another store and got …"

You know how it goes. You start talking about something and the person you are talking to takes over the conversation.

"I found a nickel on the street and—"

"I found a dime and I was just walking home after I worked all day and I was tired and I have this terrible boss but then I found a dime. It was right on the sidewalk. And last week I found a quarter and …"

"I just fell in love with the most wonderful—"

"Really, I met this person last week and I did not believe it would happen, but there was love just standing in front of me and we connected right away and you would not believe how unusual this was because …"

"I died last night."

"Well, I died yesterday and … What did you say?"

Open Eyes, Open Head, Count on Luck

The End of Any Road Is Just the Beginning

There was the house on Victoria Drive that has a hundred knick-knacks in the front yard. Some are pinwheels spinning in the wind, some are flags flapping in that same commodity and some are strips of tinsel glimmering in the sunlight.

There must be a neat person inside.

I knocked on the door, but no one answered. Darn.

Okay, move on.

There was the fellow carrying a single long-stemmed rose who was going to the airport to meet his girlfriend who he had not seen in six months. Beautiful.

But he was in a hurry. Darn. Move on.

There was no one at Trout Lake, which seemed impossible, but it was true. There are always people at Trout Lake. Good people. Interesting.

It was there that I met Mona, who drives every day from New Westminster to have lunch at one particular picnic table. Under it are the ashes of her husband who she is very angry at for dying because she loved him so much.

And it is there that I met Reilly, who changed my life. He was the autistic ten-year-old who believed he could catch a fish in a lake that had no fish.

After I talked to him I started believing in the impossible. It never fails. I'll tell you about him again soon.

But on this day no one was there. Darn. Move on.

An hour had passed since we started. Our goal, as always, was just to find something, anything, really anything that had something of some value or interest. It should not be hard.

But some days it is impossible.

"Let's try Commercial Drive."

That's me talking. I make pronouncements like that to pretend I am giving input, but really Commercial Drive just happened to be close by.

We tried Norman's Fruit & Salad market. Norman ran the store for fifteen years then sold it to his employees and retired. He got bored of not working and was hired back by the people who used to work for him.

Nice story.

He left a few minutes before we got there. Darn. Move on.

The impossible sometimes seems impossible, which is a scary thought. So I will not have that thought.

A little further south we passed the sidewalk used market of whatever happens to be for sale today. Many people believe everything for sale there was stolen.

Sometimes that is true. Around Main and Hastings is what many people call a thieves' market with a hundred dealers either stealing from parked cars or stealing from each other and then trying to sell quickly whatever they have before someone else steals it from them. Advocates for the homeless call it survival street vending.

In either case, it is the economics taught in high-priced business schools. There you get an advanced degree and then try to see how you can wiggle just a little more profit out of something by curtailing or minimizing or shaving a little bit of surplus from something else, even when there was no surplus there to begin with. The business-school way is basically the Main-and-Hastings way except you wear better clothes.

On the sidewalk on Commercial near Broadway was something I have seen a few times, but not often: books for sale. Books lined up, standing up, showing their front covers just like in a book store, but these were on the pavement.

"Maybe," I thought, "just maybe, we will do it." Then I thought, "No. Probably stolen." Although I have no idea where they could have been stolen from. Maybe they came from the back of a thrift store, or out of some neighbourhood trading library where folks put up a box and encourage their neighbours to pick up or drop off a book.

Move on. Around the centre of the city again. I wanted something uplifting. I wanted something fascinating, interesting, or at least something you hadn't seen too many times before so that you could say that was a neat person you just saw on the telly. I wanted something good.

We passed a banquet hall at Commercial and Venables. It was for rent for weddings or funerals or things in between.

In 1976—that was a long time ago—I did a story about a group of volunteer grandparents. They would spend time with families that had no grannies or grampies and bring something into their lives, in theory. There was a white-haired gentleman who would spend an evening with two kids, about seven or eight years old, who were living with their mother in an apartment on the second floor of the hall. The apartment was small and neat. One of the windows looking out over the corner below was broken and held together by long strips of cellophane tape.

The mother actually wanted a free babysitter because she worked at night. The man was nice, the kids were nice. They talked and played a bit, then went to sleep. That was the story.

The mother came home. The man left. The cameraman was packing up.

The woman asked me if I wanted to see something in her bedroom.

No. Definitely no. This is the kind of stuff that leads to front page news forty years later. Besides, I was and am married. And happy.

Come on, she said.

I called the cameraman. We will both see, I said.

The woman was an exotic dancer. She took off her coat. She had on a leopard-print costume. The walls of her bedroom were covered with leopard-print wallpaper. That was enough. I wanted to leave.

I turned around.

"That's what I wanted to show you," she said.

There in a giant fish tank was an even more giant python inside sticking out its tongue.

"Nice," I said.

"My pet," she said.

There were many thoughts, mostly about symbolism, that entered my I-want-to-get-out-of-here brain. I left, having those thoughts that I did not want to have.

But I still had them because that window is still broken. You can see it. Northwest corner of the building, second floor. The building has been bought and sold several times and repainted, but the window is still held together by tape.

In my memory I had the story about the volunteer grandfather and the weirdness about the snake. So much of life is like that. Good and weird.

It has now been forty-two years and the kids probably have kids and they say to their kids, "You would not believe your grandmother."

I wish they would fix that window.

And a few blocks away is Strathcona Park. Once a cameraman and I saw a man walking around the park in the rain reading the Bible. The book was inside a clear plastic bag. It was a nice story. Eight or nine years later we saw the same man walking around the park reading the Bible, but this time the words were on an electronic thing. It was sunny. Nice story.

The cameraman, John McCarron, has since died. Sad.

There are so many memories when you go out and look for something neat. I tell people this every day. Just do that one thing, and you have a memory. When you pass by the place where you found something it will come back to you. It beats collecting bottle caps, which of course no one does any more.

We went up Main Street.

Here is another stroke of weirdness. In every city and town in the world when you go north you say you are going "up" that street. And in every city I know of, when you go "up" the numbers go up. Check it out in any city. You get on the subway at Fourteenth Street and go *up* to Forty-Second. That is pretty simple. Most people can figure it out.

In Vancouver, on the other hand, if you are at Twelfth Avenue and you want to go to First Avenue you would think you go south. Not so. You go north. Slow down. Stop reading. Think: You are going from a high number to a low number and you are going north. That's crazy.

If you want to go from Tenth Avenue to Fortieth Avenue you are going up in numbers but in Vancouver you are driving south.

I know they started numbering from False Creek. All the streets north of the water had names. So going south they used numbers. And they started at one, which is a very sensible number to begin with.

But. Somewhere along the line of history someone could have said, "Whoops. Maybe we can fix this."

In Surrey, Cloverdale, Aldergrove—sensible places—Zero Avenue begins at the border. Of course it does.

But not Vancouver. When you are going north you are going "down." When you go south you are going "up." These are things to ponder.

The city did change the names of numerous streets and avenues. Main Street was first Westminster Avenue. Then in the early twentieth century the powers that were decided they wanted to attract people— meaning Americans, meaning foreign investors, the same label the city is now having a headache over—so they changed the name of Westminster Avenue to Main Street, because every American town has a Main Street.

It did not work. Americans were coming here, but mostly for the beer. Which is another story that you read earlier. But in short if you drive over the intersection of Main and Broadway you are going over the once upon a time main water source for all the beer made in Vancouver.

It is all under asphalt now. Sad.

Again, if you collect stories, from meeting people, from books, newspapers, friends, you really can't go anywhere without saying, "Wow. You know what happened here?"

But be careful of going on too long. Then folks will say, "Can't we talk about the Canucks?"

So, I stop now. But now you have these stories to add to your collection.

Meanwhile: "Let's go back to Commercial and talk to the book-seller," I said. Because we were running out of time and places.

We headed to Broadway and Commercial and I worried that he might be gone. I don't want another darn.

There were many people at the corner, getting on and off buses, going to the SkyTrain or looking for someone selling drugs. It is an interesting corner.

There were T-shirts hung from a fence, jewellery on blankets on the ground and a bicycle for sale. I felt sorry for the fellow who did not lock up his bike yesterday.

"Are you the bookseller?" I asked a tall, powerful fellow.

"No, that's him over there."

I said thanks and went to him over there.

The bookseller did not want to be on television. He does not have a permit, he said. I thought no one had a permit. He was worried about people in bookstores getting angry at him. Then he said he likes my books. They sell fast. I am happy. You could be happy, or unhappy, knowing you could find my books on the sidewalk going for two dollars. But as far as a story goes, no.

Darn.

I turned around. I asked the tall and powerful fellow what he sells.

T-shirts, he said. Would you tell me about them, I asked.

"I'd rather tell you about my anniversary."

"How long you've been here?" I asked.

"How long since I didn't die from an overdose," he said.

"How does this happen?" I thought. The treasure was right here.

His name was Doug. Two years ago, almost to this day, he was with two friends and he took some new drug. He did not know what it was.

He had been ingesting chemicals for more years than he could remember. And he did not care what this new drug was, he said. He just wanted something to get high, or stay high, or whatever that feeling is that he wanted more than life.

A few moments later he was in blackness. He remembered nothing. He was told later that his friend's girlfriend called 9-1-1 and gave him artificial respiration.

Doug opened his jacket. "See this blue shirt?" It was a T-shirt like some of those he was selling, except it was blue. "The medics told me that was my colour. They said I was so close to not coming back that it was a miracle."

He said that while he was in the hospital he thought of the people he would never have seen again. He thought of the friends who would not have been surprised, and the friends who would have forgotten about him.

He did not like either of those thoughts.

He called his mother and told her he would not do drugs again.

This was his second anniversary.

His T-shirts were not stolen. He bought them from a friend who sold them in bundles, he said.

He was smiling. It was the uplifting moment I was looking for. And it was right here where I did not want to go.

What Did You Say?

Language Was Invented So One Person Could Confuse Another

We change. I know that. My mother did not understand me. Your mother did not understand you.

That is a given.

But then I was in a park in East Vancouver.

It is a heroic, different, unbelievable park. It is the only, the *only* time I have known the government to give in to the local population.

The park is at Brunswick and East Eighth.

Someone told me about it and I had no idea where Brunswick is or was. And I have spent most of my adult life cruising Vancouver.

It was right there. You see. Look. Right there, one block north of Kingsgate Mall, which no one in Vancouver goes to except for the thousands who shop there.

The mall is dark and gloomy. It is not a mall like a mall should be. It is small and claustrophobic, not the way malls are usually made.

It is owned by the Vancouver School Board. Something about that makes sense.

Why don't they sell it and brighten up some classrooms? No comment.

Two short blocks north of the mall is a park. Trees, grass, the usual stuff. It is Guelph Park.

One day someone who is creative made a cedar statue of a reclining figure doing nothing.

Twenty-one years later, another artist put up a sign that said "Dude Chilling Park."

The statue looked like a dude chilling. It's half-modern and half-understandable, and half-chilling and half-dude. And the sign looked just like the signs the Park Board makes except on it there was a new name: "Dude Chilling Park." You can imagine what the Park Board thought.

Next day the sign was taken down.

Next day the sign went back up: "Dude Chilling Park."

Let us jump ahead past the craziness of people versus government and just let you know there was a petition, and eighteen hundred people in this newly up-and-coming place transitioning out of a worn-out neighbourhood into a vibrant one where young people and students and people who wanted to live in a place that was looked down on and now is one of the new *in* places, said yes to the new name.

They won.

So it is, officially, Dude Chilling Park.

Or at least a corner of the old Guelph Park is the new Dude Chilling Park, which is a bureaucratic way of giving in without looking like you're giving in.

And I am standing in front of the sign and I do not know what to do. I cannot tell you what a dude is. I think it is someone who is like a beatnik in the 1950s who has a goatee and drinks little cups of coffee and listens to jazz and says, "Yeah, man. Cool."

I knew them, but I did not understand what cool was. And I liked bigger cups of coffee.

Or it could have been someone in the 1970s who had long hair and smoked strange cigarettes and listened to protest songs against the war and said they were digging it.

I was against the war. I did not smoke those cigarettes—beer was better. And I did not understand what digging was.

Now I am standing in front of that sign that says "Chilling." I don't understand chilling.

Wait, someone is walking on the sidewalk. He is right in the corner of the picture being gathered by the cameraman. This is wonderful. He might be an expert in chilling. The press gets its authorities anywhere it can.

"Hello. Hate to bother you, we are from …" You know the rest.

"Can I ask you please, what makes a dude a dude?"

Young fellow, without hesitation, without referring to notes or Google, says, "It's your level of chilling."

This is deeper than I had hoped.

"Okay, how do you chill?" I ask.

"It depends, but if you're a dude, you chill."

This is close to Buddhism or *Dr. Phil* or something. And I am happy with the answer. It explains everything just like "cool" or "digging," which explained everything without explaining anything.

Politicians excel at this, but using five- and six-syllable words.

I ask his name. Grant. He leaves. I am happy. I understand nothing but at least I understand that there is an answer that explains nothing, as in some corporate boardroom meetings.

Grant leaves us, walking away, talking to himself, no, actually arguing with himself. We can see this. His arms, his hands each sticking out from his sides moving up and down, weighing something, then both hands with thumbs up decide on something.

He turns and runs—yes, runs—back to us. This must be important.

For the first time I see he is wearing sneakers and it is January and this I know is trendy with people who are dudes.

"I know some pretty gnarly dudes," he says.

This is wonderful, I think. I still don't know what a dude is and now I am going to maybe not learn what a gnarly dude is.

"What's a gnarly dude?" I ask.

"It's guys who are really radical," he says.

"What does that mean?"

"Radical is your level of …" and then he pauses so he can explain this in a way he hopes I might, possibly, understand.

"Like the more radical you are the higher level of stoked you become."

My shoulders drooped. I sighed. But I did not shout or show exasperation in my question, I did not scream "WHAT ARE YOU TALKING ABOUT?" I just simply asked, "What does 'stoked' mean?"

We are at the PhD level now. We are splitting the atoms of words. Grant is my splitter.

"'Stoked' grows from a fire."

Now, at last, a noun I understand. Fire. I have no idea where this is going but I know what fire is and I am happy, until he adds:

"You know what I mean, you stoke the fire."

"Okay," a very quiet *okay*, is my contribution to this world of fire and stoked and chilling and dudes in a park of grass and trees.

"But if you look at a group of people as a fire …"

"Yes," I say slowly as though I understand but really just to let Grant know I am still conscious.

"You're stoking!" he says while moving his arms as though he were stoking a fire. He is in charge of the orchestra and this is the symphony of gnarly, stoking fire. He is beaming.

Then I ruined it all by asking if this had something to do with being a dude or chilling.

"Yeah, I mean *yeah*! If you're a real dude you get super radical and then you're stoked."

"Can you stoke in this park?" I ask.

He looks at me like I have missed everything he has taught.

"I've gotten stoked here, right here," he says. But there is something in his face that says to me, "You poor dude, you will never be stoked because let's face it, you are not radical, so how could you possibly chill?"

Then he leaves.

I look at the sign that says "Dude Chilling Park" and think it's still nice here even if you just sit. Okay, maybe you can chill just a bit while you are sitting—that is, if you want to be a dude. But avoid being too radical, because you don't want to get stoked when you are trying to relax in what is actually a quiet, peaceful, otherwise ordinary park.

The Teenager's Ears

Hearing What You Want to Hear No Matter What Is Said

She said, "Take out the garbage."
He heard "Blah blah the barbage."
I can't Blah blah the barbage
Because I don't know how to blah,
And I don't know what barbage is.
She said, "Did you hear me?"
He said, "What'd you say?"
She said, "The garbage!"
He said, "In a minute. When I finish what I'm doing."
She heard, "Minish, fishing, bluing."
I don't understand him.
I don't understand her.
But just wait a few years. It will pass
And your no-longer-a-teenager will say:
"I don't understand those kids."

Seen and Appreciated

Remember Just One Thing and It Will Be Everything to Everyone

Oprah made me write this.

Oprah had been on CNN. She was saving the world and in truth, she was doing a good job. She talked about Donald Trump and war and poor people and some of the people she has met and helped and how she was *not* running for president.

She is amazing. I do not think anyone will ever find something bad about her except that her childhood poverty was worse than she has talked about and her love of people is more than she has expressed.

That, of course, makes no sense. It is not bad to love more than anyone knows.

Okay, I like her.

In the interview on CNN she said something, not about wars and pain and overcoming hardship, but she said, "What people want is recognition, to be noticed, to be accepted."

"*Yes,*" I thought.

I had heard that somewhere else just the day before. It is a very simple bit of deep philosophy.

We all want to be noticed. We all want others to know we are here. We do not want to be famous or rich or admired. Okay, wrong. We do want that. But in our simple, private worlds we mostly want someone to say "Hello," followed by our name.

That is all.

The day before I saw Oprah's interview I was in Donald's Market on East Hastings near Nanaimo. I went to visit a wonderful checkout clerk named Carmen. She memorizes names.

When I first met her four years earlier, she had five thousand names in her head. You probably have five. Okay, I have wronged you. You have ten. Maybe twenty.

Honest to heaven, Carmen knew five thousand names. They were her regular customers and her once-in-a-while customers. They were delivery people who come with apples and oranges. They were folks who come once a week and once a month. They were everyone who passes in front of her.

"Hi, what's your name?"

"Nicole."

"Hello, I am Carmen."

Carmen had never seen Nicole before. She may never see her again. She bought some green onions and squash.

Nicole left the checkout lane and went out the door. Before the door closed Carmen grabbed a notebook and wrote, "5,086: Nicole. Green onions and squash. Tall, grey hair."

If Nicole walked into Donald's Market six months later, Carmen would look at her. Tall. Grey hair. As she approached the cash register Carmen would run through the Rolodex, the notebook, in her mind.

Tall, grey hair. Green onions and squash.

"Hello, Nicole."

"How did you remember my name?"

"I just do," Carmen will say. "You are important to me."

And Nicole will feel good. I could say that in other ways, but that is the basic idea. She will feel good and there is no better feeling in life.

Carmen says that writing someone's name in her book is her crutch. Once the name is in there she does not have to worry about forgetting it. If she sees someone and cannot remember their name she knows it is in the book and it comes back to her.

It is a simple process and it works. Try it. Try it with anything. Write it and you will remember it.

She saw the tall woman with grey hair.

"No green onions today, Nicole?"

"How did you remember that? How did you remember my name?"

"You are special."

Wow. Can you imagine how good the tall woman with grey hair and green onions felt?

Four years later I went back to Donald's Market.

I asked, "How many names?"

Carmen smiled. "Ten thousand."

This is totally unbelievable. No one on earth can remember ten thousand names.

"I am up to book five," she said. And she pulled out from under her counter two books. One had number four on it, and the other, five.

"Actually I am past ten thousand. I'm up to 10,046."

Of course. But this is not an audit.

For the story I asked, who is that? And she told me who that was. And who that? And she told me. And that? Again.

Then came a fellow, heavy-set. Their greeting, "Hello, Mikhail." A Russian name.

"Tell me something about yourself," I asked Mikhail.

"I speak Russian, Turkish, Hebrew, French, Spanish and English," he said. And I thought, "Of course, who doesn't?"

And after Carmen mentioned his name, I asked, "How does she make you feel?"

That is the most common and trite question ever. But his answer was the most profound.

"It makes me feel I am someone. And isn't that what we all want?"

Yes. That is what we all want. We want to be recognized as someone. So simple. And it can be done so simply by remembering someone's name. And that someone becomes Someone. And that Someone goes home with his bread and milk and green onions as Someone.

Oprah gets it and Carmen gets it.

Carmen is a saint. She works at a cash register, but she recognizes ordinary people and makes them feel like someone.

Try it. You would make someone's day. Just get a notebook.

And if you go to Donald's Market, don't forget. Her name is Carmen.

"How did you know that?" she may ask.

Gender Neutral

A Butterfly by Any Other Name Could Start an Argument

M aybe we have gone too far. On the other hand, maybe we are just getting started.

Granted, it is bad to make girls play only with dolls and boys play only with cap shooters. We are past that, right?

For hundreds, thousands of years, women cleaned, picked up after others, had babies, and solved problems. Then they grew the garden, not the flower garden but the vegetable garden, which kept the family alive.

And they dried tears, gave hugs and made the beds and, well, you know, they did everything while the men went to work and did ... what?

They did the stuff of going to work, which women were often not allowed to do.

Jump ahead a few centuries. Women do that work now as well as men, and in many cases go home and do the other work too.

And now we are up to today. Boys and girls should be equal.

Yes.

Boys and girls should get the same breaks.

Yes.

Boys and girls should get names that do not label them as boys and girls.

Uh oh.

Girls and boys know this. The ones who are in elementary school, the ones who will run the world in less than twenty years, know this. They don't flinch at gender-neutral names.

And some of them have now become crusaders.

There was a group of girls and boys at Trout Lake. And they saw a monarch butterfly that was in distress and hovering near the sand on a tiny beach next to the lake.

Canada geese were trying to poke at it, but the butterfly was safe. The geese were so fat from the kind people who fed them that they could not move their swollen bellies fast enough to get the butterfly.

Some kids surrounded the beautiful insect. One scooped his hands under it and brought it back to a crowd of mothers and kids sitting on a log.

"What should we call it?" one asked.

They have to name it because they have it, a human trait.

One tried to stroke its wings.

"Don't do that," said another one. "They have some powder on their wings or something that helps them fly."

"They look so soft."

"Let's call it Boris," said a girl.

"Boris is a boy's name," said a boy.

"No, it's a girl's name," said a girl.

"Let's call it Buttercup," said a boy.

"But Buttercup is a girl's name," said a girl.

"It could be a boy's name if the boy was sure of his gender identity," said a boy who had been listening too closely to his parents who were ahead of the curve.

"What does that mean?" asked a girl.

"I don't know, but my parents say if we can solve the problem of gender identity we can solve the problems of the world. And that's what I want to do."

All the kids were quiet. They were listening to words they did not understand. The mothers who were with the kids were quiet. They were listening to words that made them wonder if they were not being parental enough.

The butterfly flapped his/her wings and took off.

"Goodbye, Boris," said some.

"Goodbye, Buttercup," said some.

And the butterfly flew down to the ground where a goose almost got it, and the kids shrieked, and I shrieked.

Then it flew up and over some bushes, which was good, no matter what his/her name is, or was, or should be.

"What does gender whatever mean?" asked a girl.

"I don't know," said the boy. "I think it means a butterfly can be a boy or a girl."

"So it can be Boris," said the girl. And they started again.

"No, that's a boy's name," said the boy. "It should be Buttercup."

"But that's a girl's name."

"Is not," said the boy.

"Is so," said the girl.

"Is not," said the boy.

The mothers told them to stop.

And at that moment Boris Buttercup flew back toward them. We have video of it.

"Why don't we just call it Butterfly," said one little kid.

The other kids, the bigger kids, stopped arguing for a second while the thought of a new name flew into their heads and the real butterfly flew over those same heads. They did not have a conversation or discussion or question period or vote, just suddenly:

"Goodbye, Butterfly. Good luck, Butterfly."

The Ladder

You Can Always Pay a Lot for a Lesson That Is Free

I don't need help. No, I don't need someone to hold the ladder. I've done this for years. I'm fine. Don't worry.

I'm a guy. I don't need help.

No, I'm fine. Yes, it's raining so I have to hurry.

Every time I go up there I say I can see forever, or at least I can see inside the rain gutter, which is clogged forever. You've been there. You know.

I love it up here. One more time, up, yes, it's raining harder, but the gutter needs cleaning.

Up, up, like Superman. One more rung and then quicker than a wink. No, a wink is too slow.

Faster than anything that you know which is fast, the bottom of the ladder slips backward.

I go down and watch the ground come up. I think: "Darn."

Ladder hits the ground. I think I hear it crash. It's a metal ladder. The rungs hit the deck and I hit the rungs, the hard metal rungs, which leave dents in my body.

My shoulder is dislocated, broken, and the tendon ripped out.

Pain and more pain and emergency room and long, long—you know it—long wait for an operation and then pain, again.

Lesson one: Very simply, at a certain age, try to avoid being stupid.

When you are young, you supposedly bounce. When you are older, you don't.

Lesson two: Find someone to hold the ladder no matter how embarrassing that is. And say thank you. It won't hurt a bit.

Riding the Bus

Luxury Is How You Look at It

A fter I broke my shoulder I could not drive.

I kept saying, "Sure, I can drive. One hand is good enough."

But my wife and the doctor said, "What are you thinking?" That's like saying, "Are you nuts? You went up a ladder in the rain. Look what happened. Now you are going to drive with one hand? What are you thinking?"

But I often drive with one hand. Who doesn't?

But suppose it is a dark and stormy night, and there is a detour around a construction site that you do not see, and you cannot turn fast enough with one hand to avoid driving into a freshly dug hole in the ground, and you have to call a tow truck, and this makes you late for dinner. What are you going to do then?

Okay, you have a point.

And suppose while your one hand is steering you merge on the highway when suddenly one of your front tires has a blowout and you swerve and bang into a passing police car?

Okay, another point.

And suppose your one hand …

Oh, forget it. I won't drive.

So I am standing at a bus stop waiting for the large metal container with someone else at the wheel. I will soon be thinking this is my personal limo, with fifty-four of my close friends sharing the ride.

I will be thinking that after I get on the bus and read it on an advertising slogan inside the bus.

Those advertising writers are pretty good.

"Hello," she says. She is the driver.

Okay, I'll give it a try. I have not been on a bus for years.

"Hello."

"What happened to you?" She says.

"Don't ask," I say, "because then I will have to tell you I fell off a ladder and you will say, 'what were you doing up a ladder?'"

She says without saying, "At your age, what are you doing up a ladder?" She does not add, "That's stupid," which is kind of her, but I hear it anyway.

And then I wonder if she is just going to sit here talking or drive. I am such a pragmatist.

And she says, "I'm sorry. Hope you get better quick."

That was nice. Her name is Elaine. She has become my personal chauffeur. I've never had one of those.

I sit down, but I do not take the seats for people with disabilities because that would be inconsiderate.

But I cannot get into a side seat. I have my book bag, and although it really only holds my lunch in it and no books, it takes up room and I am holding it with my left hand and my right hand is useless and I am trying to slide into a seat, but you really need one hand to hold onto the seat in front because there is no room to get in if you don't. I sit between the seats. Luckily they are stuck together.

And then I realize Elaine has not driven off. She is waiting until I am sitting. She is kind, even if she's behind schedule.

If you see anyone in a wheelchair or on crutches or walking with a cane or with a guide dog or with a baby, or two babies, or if they are very old, or very large, or carrying an extra bag of groceries, or if their arm is in a sling because they fell off a ladder, try to be as kind as Elaine was to me.

Anyway, I am on this bus which goes along East Hastings Street, and many people who get on fit into all of the categories above, and many more do not pay, and some are loud and obnoxious. And the driver keeps driving without losing her temper or speeding up or stopping too quickly or honking, except when someone literally jumps in front of the bus. Elaine honks out of instinct, but it is just a quick, harmless honk. And then that person sticks his finger out at her and she does nothing else but waits until he walks on.

And then we leave that area and some passengers who are getting off start saying, "Thank you." It is not a special thing. I can tell it is what they say every day. And then more and then most of them are saying thank you.

And each time Elaine says, "You're welcome."

I get off and do what the others did. "Thank you," I say.

"Hope you get better," she says.

One more incident, one out of many that could be turned into a television series. Wait a minute. Someone did that a while ago, *On the Buses*, a British sitcom. And now I knew where they got their scripts.

Here's another.

A driver named Doug is going past the old police station on Main Street. The police station is now closed, and the front has turned into a homeless camp. There is something beyond strange about that.

A man walks across the middle of the street in front of Doug's bus. Doug stops. The man walks around to the door and taps on it. Doug opens the door.

The man climbs up and says he has no money. Doug says that's okay.

The man asks where the bus is going. Doug tells him on Main to Pender. The man asks if he passes any restaurants on the way.

Doug says he doesn't know and pulls off. The bus goes two blocks and the man shouts: "There's a restaurant!" Doug pulls over at the next stop.

The man says the restaurant is back there. He points half a block behind them. The door opens and he gets off, saying bad words because Doug did not stop back there.

I get off soon after that and tell Doug he has great patience. He says, "It's easy. There is no alternative." So right, so simple. Patience works better than blood pressure medicine.

And now, long after my arm has healed, I am still riding the buses. I know there are some drivers who do not wait for someone running for their bus, but most are outstanding. And most have as much patience as driving skills, which they have a lot of. If the Bible were rewritten it would have bus drivers in it. Or at least bus drivers should teach meditation classes on the side.

On a bus you pay for the ride, but everything you ever wanted to know about psychology, religion, understanding, strength, kindness and the variants of social evolution, you get as a bonus. And it beats reading tweets.

The Couple

If You Don't Try Something Nothing Will Happen

A cameraman, Gary Rutherford, says, "Why don't we do a story about that car passing by?"

"Why?"

"Because look at the dents. Maybe they have a story about the dents."

Gary is wise. He sees potential in everything. I see disaster, because if we catch up to the person with the dented fenders and if I jump out of Gary's SUV at a red light and if I run up to the car and if I say, "Why do you have dented fenders?" I know the person with the dented fenders will step on the gas, and maybe run over my foot.

That's what I think.

But to be honest I jumped out of another camera truck, at a red light (yes, at a red light, of course, I am not a complete idiot, just idiot enough to try to catch up to a truck several cars ahead of us waiting at the same light) and talked to the driver and explained that I would like it if he pulled over on the next block so we could talk about the stuffed teddy bear on his back bumper.

I did this on one of my first days at CTV and the driver stopped and presto, there was a story about a teddy bear living on a bumper. Easy. So doing stupid and dangerous things does work.

And in the last book I told you about getting out of another camera truck and running up to an old postal van that had a wishing well on its side and then finding myself staring at a mannequin of a witch staring back at me through the side window.

That was a beautiful story.

But now I am a year older and it is getting harder to catch up to a car with dents in its fender, so I say, "No."

Then Gary says, "Look at those two sitting at that bus stop. They're not moving. Surely you can catch up to them."

This is verbatim conversation on the pursuit of most stories on most days.

Two people waiting for a bus is a bad idea because the bus will be coming in a few minutes. Bad because I have to introduce myself, tell them what we are doing, ask them about themselves and hope they say something interesting, and then get pictures of them. And again, the bus is coming.

It is good because they are old and just sitting there. What more could anyone hope for?

I jump out. Gary looks for a parking spot. I have the easier job.

"Hello." The usual, "Hello. Don't want to bother you but you two look beautiful."

In truth, they did.

"It's none of my business." I say that often because it is the truth, and sometimes they say, "You're right."

That gives me a chance to escape before they punch me in the nose for asking something that is none of my business.

And sometimes they say, "Yes?" with a big question mark. They are saying that while thinking, "He's going to ask for money." "He's going to invite us to join his church." "He's going to get us involved in a pyramid scheme but because we will be among the first to join he will make us rich. Okay, say hello to him."

They say, "Yes?"

"I was wondering," I start to say when the woman, Marilyn, interrupts. "You were wondering if we've been together for a long time. No, we haven't."

"Well, it's sixteen years," says the man, Frank. "That's a long time."

"It doesn't matter how long," I say. "You still look beautiful, like you have just met."

"We met at a seniors' centre," says Marilyn. "Over a Ping-Pong game."

They were both single after funerals.

"He was cute," says Marilyn.

Frank rolls his eyes, which is the perfect thing for a tough old guy to do.

"Do you remember the first time you said you liked her?" I ask Frank.

I am hoping for something sweet.

"I do," says Frank.

"I don't," says Marilyn.

And then Frank pauses.

"Oh, that," says Marilyn.

"Oh, what?" I ask.

There is a line growing for the bus. It is coming. Please say something. And please say something wonderful and memorable and please don't say "We can't tell you," which so many other people would be saying at this moment. Please.

"I asked her, how's her sex life?" says Frank.

"I told him it was none of his business," says Marilyn, who is smiling with a shy smile. Her smile is hard to describe. She liked what he said, obviously. But it was their secret. Then she seemed to like that the secret was out.

All of this I am guessing from two upturned corners of her lips, but I think you would think the same thing if you saw her smile.

There is movement all around us. The bus is coming. It is one red light away.

"Can I ask how old you are?" That is me desperately trying for something that will put it into perspective. They look elderly, but if they are in their late sixties or early seventies it would have less impact.

"I'm eighty-six," says Marilyn.

"I'm eighty-two," says Frank.

"I robbed the cradle," says Marilyn.

Then the bus pulls up and they get up and some younger people are kind and step aside while they climb on board.

The only pictures we had were the two of them talking. The two of them holding hands. The two of them sitting together. The two of them climbing on a bus and the bus pulling away.

What more could anyone ask for?

The story was so easy to edit. We just put together the pictures and words of what happened. Two people, one love story.

But what do I say at the end? I have no idea. They got on a bus and left.

I want to say something profound, something that will give others hope, something that will be memorable and change the world. Okay, or at least something that sounds good.

I try this and that and the other thing. I try changing the words around. I try Shakespearean and classical thoughts of finding youth a second time.

The editor, Kim Cirillo, who is patiently recording each line and then erasing it after I shake my head, or after she shakes her head, says, "They are just two kids in love. Maybe you can say something about that?"

Brilliant, wonderful, superb, simple! It is what you see, and what you don't see. Editors are good with things like that.

I take the microphone and say, "They got on their chariot, just two kids in love," as the bus pulls away.

It was the best story of the week.

What I learned was:

Listen to your camera operator, wife, husband, kids, friends. When they have an idea, take it. Did you have a better idea?

Don't worry if you do not have enough time to do something. Do it anyway. Darn, I could have done that if I knew I had that much time.

Hope for surprises. Almost every breathing human person has them.

Listen to your editor, wife, husband, etc. I think I just said this, but it is worth saying again. Editors don't get their names on things, they just make them better. Sometimes they are better than the ones who get the credit.

Is That Really Me?

Here Is a Mystery No One Can Solve

They are different people, these people whose pictures I am looking at.

They could not be the same person.

They look different. But they have the same name, same start date. Same end date. Two pictures, one obituary.

One: beautiful, round cheeks. Pretty smile, much hair and blue eyes.

Two: wrinkled cheeks, pleasant smile, sparse hair and blue eyes.

Between the two, sixty or seventy years of pain, fun, love, falling in, falling out.

Babies, diapers, working, not working.

Tragedy, triumph. Jumping down stairs, holding on down the stairs.

Two pictures.

One life. Same person. But neither would believe that other person could be the same person, which is a completely different person.

Be patient with the old and young because if the old you stood alongside the young you, you would each think the other was impossible to understand.

Benny's Market

What You Have Left After You Lose Everything Is Everything

Once upon a time, long ago, Strathcona was an Italian neighbourhood. That was long ago. Then it became a Chinese neighbourhood. And the Italians moved out. People like to live with people who look like themselves. That is a hardship of getting people to live together.

But leave that aside.

Benny's Market at Union and Princess was in the middle of Vancouver's Little Italy in 1918.

Italians were in Strathcona in the early twentieth century and the area went from Union ... Okay, you don't know where Union is. It starts at Main and goes east, and it was all Italian, and poor. Then it was Black and poor, then Chinese and poor.

Now it is trendy, white and rich. Very rich. Who else could afford to live in a formerly poor neighbourhood? The white and rich are turning it into a remodelled neighbourhood of gardens and coffee shops and art galleries.

I learned about Benny's Market when cameraman Jim Fong said we had to go there because it was so neat. I had never heard of it. Jim took me inside.

"Hello, I haven't seen you for a long time."

That was the Chinese woman behind the counter who went to school with Jim.

I can tell you that when you are being taken on a tour by someone who grew up in the neighbourhood you get insight better than any guidebook.

The neighbourhood is not like it was when Jim was a kid. If you don't like where you live, stick around for a few generations and it will change.

But back before Jim was there, Italians were there in the hundreds, maybe thousands.

And they wanted Italian food. Who doesn't? So they went to Benny's Market. It had salami and cheese and pasta and pastries.

A man name Alfonso Benedetti, who came from Italy, opened Benny's Market in 1918. And he did well, even though he worked seven days a week. And he married the girl across the street who came to buy candy.

"Marry him," her mother said. "He has a food store. You'll never go hungry."

Time passed. His son, Ramon, was born and later took over the store. That is a quick leap of forty years. It skips the time of Ramon the boy sleeping in the back of the store, and sneaking out to play with his friends in the back alley before his mother said, "Get in here and do some work."

And it skips the time of Ramon going to school and working behind the counter making salami sandwiches. And it skips when the Depression left many without money and Ramon's father said, "Anyone who is hungry and comes in here we will give a salami sandwich free of charge."

It skips all that.

And then Ramon the boy became Ramon the man who had a son, also Ramon, who grew up in the store like his father.

And the neighbourhood started changing, but it was still poor.

And the father told the son what his father had told him: "If someone comes in and has no money and says he is hungry, give them some salami and bread. No charge."

But that is not the story.

When the Chinese moved in they bought Italian food.

And Ramon's son, Ramon Jr., married a Chinese schoolmate, Janet. She decorated the store with Chinese things along with Italian things, and around them mega-supermarkets were opening but Benny's Market kept going. And Janet went to school with Jim the cameraman. The world is so snug.

And the elder Ramon had a dispute with Coca-Cola about the condition of the Coca-Cola sign out front of his store.

It needed repairs and paint.

Coke said no.

Ramon said, "The hell with you."

He painted over the sign with dark-green paint.

He would have used black but he said he did not have any.

The big bottle cap that previously said "Coke" became a green dot which said nothing. Or maybe it said something strong and unprintable.

"Boy, they were upset," said Ramon.

But that is not the story.

Now jump ahead several decades.

Ramon Sr. is still working while his son and daughter-in-law have largely taken over the store.

But Ramon Sr. got a scratch on his foot. No problem. We all get that, sometimes. But his scratch got infected.

In short, he lost his right leg.

"I'll just be a bit slower," he said from his wheelchair.

No complaining. Just reaching up now to the counter instead of down to the counter to make salami sandwiches.

Three years later he lost his left leg.

"Won't be chasing the girls anymore," he said. "Or riding on a skateboard."

Ha ha ha.

He really made you laugh. A real "ha ha ha." And he was laughing in the face of a bully, an attacker, a heartless thief who stole his legs. And he laughed some more. He is eighty-eight, in a wheelchair and still working.

That is the story.

Junk Shop

Everything Is There, if You Look Right There

It was a sad day when the last junk shop closed on Main Street. That was Abe's Junk at Main and Twenty-Eighth. The street had become trendy and junk was replaced by boutique.

Boutique usually does not have character or spice and especially not a story behind it.

"Hey, over there," says cameraman Gary Rutherford. He says it loudly.

I am looking not there, but over there, the opposite there.

"What?"

"Don't know, but I thought I saw something."

He circles the block, parks, gets out and stares across the street. I do the same and see nothing.

"What?" I ask, conserving words.

"I thought there was a guy standing in front of that shop with a hockey jersey on."

This would not be unusual. On this day many are wearing jerseys to honour the young hockey players killed in Saskatchewan.

But I see nothing. Gary crosses the street and stops at a junk shop. This is amazing to me because I did not know there was a junk shop there despite more than thirty years of reporting on Main Street.

If someone you know says they do not see something that is right under their nose, but you see it, do not be annoyed or superior or sarcastic.

We go inside and there is the man with the hockey jersey. It is red, which is why Gary saw it, and since it is red it was from Montreal. If you did not know this, pretend you did because almost everyone else in the country knows it.

The man with the shirt is Bob, and he says he has had this shop for forty-one years.

"What?" I think. "This is impossible. This could not be."

I will tell you why in a moment.

First we talk to Bob about his jersey. He has not worn it for twenty years. He got it when he went to the Pacific Coliseum with his father to watch the Canadiens play the Canucks.

"Who did you cheer for?" I ask.

Bob looks down at his jersey and asks in a patient way, "Who do you think?"

He says in the 1980s half the Vancouver hockey fans rooted for Montreal. That was Canada's team.

Then he shows us around his shop. He has an eight-track player and signs, old signs: "Eat Wonder Bread," "Indian Motorcycle." And he has hand-sized models of robots he made himself out of scrap material.

One was made of a coffee pot. Another, from the keys of a typewriter. Neat.

He says he wore his jersey in honour of the junior hockey players who perished.

It is a sweet, touching story. Thank you, Gary.

But the other story, the one not on the air, was about the Main Street that once was and is no more. It was a street richly characterized by junk shops. And then they were gone.

They were wonderful, especially Abe's.

His shop was a collection of everything you could ever hope to find or did not know existed and then you could have it for, "What? No way!"—not expensive. So cheap. So you bought it.

Abe was from Poland. He was Jewish. He had been in a concentration camp. He had a number tattooed on his arm. He was a beautiful person.

"Junk is good," he told me. "Everything is good if you want it to be."

He was a gentle philosopher with white hair and a broad chest. He came to Canada after the war and began picking up junk when people put out their garbage.

He had a child's wagon which he would pull and fill, and then he'd try to sell what he had found.

That led to his shop. I went there so many times his wife gave me a necklace for my wife. It was costume jewellery, but it was a gift and it was beautiful.

I brought my wife to meet them. It was all warm and lovely.

Next door to him was Morris's Junk Shop. Morris had also been through the camps and had suffered and survived, or sort of survived.

He collected things and he put them in his shop. He put so many things in his shop he had no room to go inside.

The fire department made him close up several times. Then he would clean up a bit and reopen. And then fill his shop again.

If you squeezed in and found a lamp you wanted to buy, you would ask Morris, "How much?"

He would take the lamp from you, look over it carefully, then put it back on its shelf.

"That's not for sale," he would say.

Pick up a toaster and he would say, "That's not for sale either."

Somehow he made a living, but basically he was a hoarder. He seldom smiled.

Abe was always laughing, so I spent most of my time with him. When he retired his son took over and hung a sign over the store that said "Antiques." I saw Abe leaning in his doorway after that. He was watching the store while his son was off on an errand.

"My son," he told me with a Yiddish accent, "he is too good for junk. What's wrong with junk?"

It was a Broadway musical in the making. *My Son, Not A Junk Dealer.*

"Junk gave him his food," said Abe. "Junk got him through school. Now he is too good for junk. What is wrong with him?"

We put that on television. It was a universal story of the changing world. It was the story of how distant each generation is from the past.

It was beautiful.

Then, one after another, the junk shops on Main Street closed. They turned into boutiques or antique shops. The street was heading toward Trendyville. And then when people started moving into condos, the antique furniture was too large for their small rooms.

Next came the condo furniture shops where the junk shops once were. That is when I stopped reporting on Main Street.

I told my friends. I told people who were not my friends that the old Main Street was gone because the junk shops were gone.

Years passed.

Then Gary saw the man with the jersey. His shop was, excuse me, *is* at Main and Twenty-Ninth, about one hundred steps from the ghost of Abe.

How did I miss it? I have no idea. If you or your friend can't find something, or miss seeing something, or are as blind as me who has two eyes that work, forgive them, or forgive yourself. It happens.

And if you get the chance, go into Bob's Junk Shop. You know where it is, and so do I. Look around. You will not leave quickly.

You can find the shop the same as you can find just about anything: open your eyes, open your head, walk an extra block and most of all, listen to others. Thanks, Gary.

And I found Main Street, again.

The Bench

Some Stories Never End, but That Is the Point

It was perfect. Better than that. Beautiful, different, odd, funny and nothing happened. How can you have a story when nothing happened?

They were sitting on a bench having coffee. The third bench just off Ogden Avenue, which is alongside the Maritime Museum, which is near Kitsilano Beach.

Nothing strange about that, except it was raining, and raining hard. Water dripped, no it poured, off the brims of their hats. Then he took a sip from a plastic cup and she did the same.

Each stared out at the inlet off the ocean.

Let that sit in your mind for a moment. Don't speed read on because there is nothing waiting for you. No information, no advancement of the story.

Just picture you and someone else sipping coffee and looking at a deserted beach, with some sailboats bouncing gently on the water in the rain just a few paddles from shore, and behind them the mountains, which you cannot see because of the clouds.

Take another sip. Just pretend.

Nice.

That is what they said. "It's very nice to come here and do nothing but look."

He said that, or she said that.

"We come every day."

"Every day?"

"Yes, every day."

In snow, in rain, in cold, insane.

"No, we like it. We dress for the weather."

And they sit.

They said they passed by this bench once, sat down and liked it. A few days later they came back. And a few days later they brought a Thermos of coffee. And a few days later they returned and said what a lovely way to start the day. Why do anything else?

I got in the habit of passing by the bench on my search for oddball things like people sitting on a bench.

And yes, they were there. Every day. In the rain—again, insane—yes, they were there.

They were there with coffee steaming while they poured it from a Thermos. They were there when it was warm and sunny. They were there when it was cold and cloudy. They were there in the snow, and rain and whatever is between.

"I forgot to ask, what are your names?"

"You wouldn't believe them," she said. "He is Darwin, and I am Eve."

That was a minor oddity in their lives, next to the major oddity of having coffee every morning, often in the rain, on the third bench just off Ogden Road.

A couple, with names that do not match, matched beautifully under matching rain hats doing what no other couple I have ever met has done. If you go by that bench, say hello. They will point out how pretty the never-changing, always-changing scene on the beach is and they will tell you how their namesakes could never acknowledge one another's existence.

Then they will tell you they both found their Garden of Eden, which according to Darwin did not exist, and yet he is here, drinking coffee in the garden. And they will tell you how they both evolved into being here while Eve would say there was no evolution, except here it is.

They both come from a long line of believers who disagree on everything except that this is the best place to have coffee in the morning.

Stick Figures

A Simple Answer to a Thorny Question

Evolution. That is a long, long word and big people get angry and fight
over it.

It means things change and get better.

Some people say people came from monkeys. That is evolution.

Other people say that is silly. They say people came from people.

One thing I know. My friends who are stick people, who I draw with a
pencil, have changed for the better.

When I was little my pencil friends' hands suck out from their stomachs.
But it is hard to hold things when your arms are down there.

Then my friends grew up and their arms moved up.

Up like your arms, which are way up there. You can hold things. And
throw things. And, most of all, hug things.

If someone asks you about EVOLUTION

don't say a word, just give them a hug.

And say that is your answer.

Pairing

Socks Don't Have to Match to Keep You Warm

S ometimes it is less up to the taste buds than to the advertising copy-writers to make, or at least describe, a perfect match.

Today's assignment: beer and burger, but make it sound elegant and expensive, but not too expensive.

"Harry, let me pour you some IPA. Now take a nibble of this tri-ple-roasted and tossed in chia seeds then layered with kimchi and sprinkled with balsamic vinegar hamburger.

"Is that trendy this week?"

"Don't know. Just see if it pairs with the beer.

Nibble, sip, nibble, sip. Sip.

"Nice. Their bouquets seem to blend into one beautiful floral arrangement."

"Harry, we're talking beer and burgers, not flowers and vases. Make it sound masculine."

Harry thinks. Then sips. Then thinks. Then sips. Then…

"Wait a minute, Harry. We have a new assignment. Spinach growers want us to pair their baby leaves with something."

"Did they say with what?"

"No, anything will do, so long as we use the word 'pair.'"

Nibble, nibble.

"This is tasteless."

"So pair it with something that tastes good."

Harry goes to the fridge and takes out some leftover grilled white-fish, red bell peppers, red onions and zucchini.

"But that's what everyone puts with spinach."

"So, can everyone be wrong?"

"But we are supposed to be original, innovative and sound like we know what we are doing."

Harry eats. "Not bad, but needs something."

Back to the fridge.

"This makes everything taste good, sun-dried tomato vinaigrette."

Harry pours it over the salad.

They taste.

"Perfect, except it could use some Cabernet."

"No, Harry, that's for burgers. Let's try Chardonnay."

Nibble, sip, nibble, sip, nibble, sip, sip, sip, sip.

"Leave out the Chardonnay and write the copy."

This is not the way it happened. I know this is not the way it happened. But at the supermarket I saw a package of greens with an interesting label.

The label tells you it pairs well with grilled whitefish, red bell peppers, red onions, zucchini and sun-dried tomato vinaigrette.

Such refinement, right, Harry?

Harry?

Harry, wake up.

Typewriters

Not Only Violins Make Beautiful Music

The article was in the *New York Times*, which, despite what Donald Trump says, is one of the world's best newspapers. But this article was not very good.

It was not because of the facts. The *Times* gets those right. It was the reporting of those facts. You have to understand the emotions and life of facts before you can talk about them. That's not just true in news stories, but in everything. You can't write a grocery list with just words. The items have meanings that make you hungry.

The story was an obituary of the woman who ran the last repair shop in New York for manual typewriters. The *Times* got that right.

The shortcoming of the story was that it was written by someone who is a little more than a decade younger than me and was in the transitional period between typewriters and computers. It was the era of the electric typewriter which was like a little drummer boy compared to the base drum of the manual typewriter.

What the writer of the story apparently never experienced was the music of the metal keys.

The story said famous people came into the typewriter repair shop to get their writing machines fixed. Then it named the people, and you know they are or were famous. And they all used manual typewriters.

It doesn't matter who they were. They were famous, but this is about the typewriters, not those who used them.

It said the shop was like dust left over from a time before word processors and computers. That is a very nice line. I wish I had written it.

But missing was the heart, soul and plain old orchestra of a large room full of manual typewriters coming alive when fingers pushed down on the keys and the letters attached to bits of steel went up to hit an ink-soaked ribbon before smashing that ribbon onto a piece of white paper. And the sound was a *click*. The voice of a typewriter.

As you wrote it went click, click, click. Then click click click click. Faster. Clickclickclickclick. Sometimes so fast the *click*s fell together into one *click* barely separated, almost like Morse code, which is something else you may have seen and heard once, in a movie.

And near the end of the line you were writing came a *bing*, like a high note on a piano that grabs your ears and sets off the next line of notes. The *bing* was the bell telling you that the line ended in five strokes and you had better figure out when to go to the next line.

And then you pushed the metal return bar on the top of the typewriter, pushed it hard, there was no electric motor pushing with you, you pushed it all the way to the end which made a drumming sound like … well, like a drum, which ended in a *clunk* and you started on the next line.

All that took place in a second and a half and it happened at the end of every line, twenty or so times a page and many, many times in a two-hundred-page novel. It was not noise, it was rhythm and typing.

Click, bing, clunk. Then click, click, click, fast. Bing. Clunk, louder because you were in a hurry and you wanted to get to that next line.

But the *click*s were not the same each time. Move to a different machine being used at the same time as you and it was a different song. Different violin, different sound.

Almost always your personal typing had your stamp on it. It came from the way you thought and talked. If you thought in short lines, you talked in short lines and you typed in short bursts of *click*s. But your fingers could only move so fast before slipping between the keys. That was the same as a pianist who forgot the next line but went on anyway. The finger was pulled up from between the keys and slipped back into the chords.

The clicking was everywhere. In office towers the *click*s, *bing*s and *clunk*s were in every office on every floor. In schools it was in the principal's office, solitary clicking by the secretary sending home a note about how bad you were. And it was in the tense typing classes where teachers would put a cloth over the keys and then grade you on what you put on the paper. That was more like progressive jazz than orchestral smoothness. Everyone had to take those classes except those going into automotive repair. Click, bing, clunk.

For most of my early working life, it was in newsrooms. Every desk had a typewriter—a big, heavy, black or grey giant of steel with rows of keys that you hit to make a series of levers lift and slam. Click. One more letter. Click, another letter. Click, click, click. Without end.

It was the sound of thought being put on paper. When you stopped thinking, the clicking stopped, and you were alone with your thoughts until you could think and click again.

There was also the sound of the teletype machines, the constant, uniform clicking that was transmitted over wires around the world. Teletype was the long-ago ancestor of Instagram, or Twitter, or email. It was typing at one end and receiving at other ends far away that never stopped.

Old shows taking place in newsrooms always had the sound of teletype machines in the background. But teletype machines were different than typewriters. Teletype had the same rhythm without fail, without stopping even at four in the morning. They were robotic. They were not alive. Typewriters were.

The first typewriter I used I found in the cellar of the apartment my mother and I had in New York. It was old even when I found it. It was dusty. The *J* key, the one you put your right index finger on if you know how to type in the traditional way, was yellow.

That was from the nicotine that had covered the finger of the landlord of the building who had used the machine for years. The nicotine oozed off his finger and slid in microscopic drops under the plastic cover of the key and solidified onto the heavy plastic on which the *J* was written.

I learned to type on that. Click … click … long pause while I looked for the next letter … click.

Darn. Wrong letter. What to do then? Take out the paper and throw it away? Go back and *X* out the mistake? You can't hand in a paper for school with *X*s.

Get Wite-Out, basically white paint with which you could paint over the wrong letter, wait for it to dry, then try again. Try that, you who makes ten mistakes in a twenty-word text message.

Then you get down to the last line of a perfectly written page and notice you have just written too close to the bottom without leaving a white margin of blank paper, which you were told to do.

You can't erase the entire line.

You pull out the paper, say something you should not say, then crumple it and throw it into a wastepaper basket, which is almost full. Then you put in a new sheet and start again at the top.

My daughter said when she was younger she went to bed listening to click, click, bing, clunk click, click, *bad word*, from me as she fell into sleep.

But the sound in newsrooms—not in the movies, but in life—was the music of current events, getting faster and faster as the deadline got closer. Click, bing, clunk. Click, bing, clunk. A clunk at deadline was loud and desperate.

And then came computers. And all was silent.

You work now in an office or school or newsroom where there is no noise. Fingers silent, eyes on a screen, no *click*, no *bing*, no *clunk*.

I have my old typewriter sitting on a trunk near my computer. It is grey. It is heavy. It has a sticker on it from an airline saying, "Caution: Heavy." It has many stickers, some funny, some meaningless. Two are from airlines that no longer exist.

The obituary of the typewriter woman was written by someone who had apparently never experienced a typewriter. He got all the facts, all the names right. But he left out the life. He never mentioned the clicking.

A Short Story After That Long Story

Last Christmas my grandchildren were visiting, which is better than gifts under a tree.

On the second morning they were here I woke to the most beautiful sound. A typewriter, my typewriter, the one that I used for news for ten years before computers came, and on which I wrote my first book, was alive. Ruby, then thirteen, who like most thirteen-year-olds can answer any computer question that Bill Gates cannot, was hitting the keys.

No, she was not typing. She was picking up a violin and touching the bow to the strings to see what sound came out. She was tapping on the ebony and ivory. Not music, just a single note, the sound of music awaking.

And what I heard as I lay on my pillow was yesterday, yesteryear, in my life.

I thanked her. She did not know what I was thanking her for. Then I read what she wrote.

```
            how to work a typewriter

            by ruby mccardell


    1. there is no number 1, you need to use the

       letter L.

    2. s ometimes, it doe s n,t work so you will

       h ave a few w eird spaces in your text.

    3. if you want a copy of what  you  are writing

       you will n eed to type-tg-the t ext again.

    4. you  h av e  to press hard on t he keys, but

       not too hard o r e lse it will leave spaces

       in the wo rds. (as read in number2)

    5. if t the stamp-thingys get stuck, you need

       to put your fingers in there to unstick them.

       please wash your hands afterwords .

    6. if you make a "typo", too bad beae- becaus e

       you cannot er ase what you wr ote.

    7. yo u can use n eat symbols like these: "#

       $%_&*+=¿¢¢,-baña but a typewriter does not

       have emojis.

    8. sometimes, you run out of ink.in that case,
```

My gosh. She *had* brought it back to life.

In an age when every computer line is neat and uniform it was hard for her to understand that in the typewriter age many novels and even more newspaper stories first looked just like the page she had written.

Keys jumped around, fingers slipped and when you were in a hurry, neatness was elusive.

And one thing for sure: no emojis.

By the time she got to the bottom of the page the ribbon had jammed and worn out.

It is hard to read her last line. But it sounded beautiful.

A Lesson in Writing

More Important Than the Product Is What You Call It

Rapeseed oil? Ugly name.

Use it on machines, nothing else. Never in the kitchen. Repeat: Never, never in the kitchen.

Look at the name.

But it's healthy. So? Look at the name.

Repeat: Nope, never, never.

Someone said: it comes from Canada, and it's oil. So: Can Oil! Can we call it Can Oil?

Not bad, but not right. Tweak the name a bit. See if you can come up with something better.

The writer saw Mazola in the supermarket, oil made from corn.

Idea.

Canola, oil made in Canada. Forget the bad name of the seed it comes from. Think of the good name of the country where it comes from.

And now it is in every kitchen, one of the world's best-selling cooking oils.

Use it on machines? Are you crazy? This is health food in a bottle. And from such a nice place.

All in a name.

The Storyteller

It Is Never Too Late to Remember

Y ou are fifty and want to do something new but you don't know what and you are afraid because it is pretty late to start on something that you might not have the time or talent for and then you will be wasting time so you quit.

What's the point? You have a point.

You are sixty and if you don't start something new you will never do it but then again there are folks who do start something new at sixty, often jogging, then running, and by the time they are sixty-two or sixty-three they are running marathons. That's impressive, but you hate running.

You are seventy. Oh, don't be silly. You're not going to start anything new. You would probably die before you got to the first step and besides isn't it time for you to sit back and do nothing? It is that time, isn't it?

Rosemary Hawkins was eighty-seven when she took a writing course.

Rosemary has much white hair and a big smile and she said she had never done any writing, none at all, besides grocery lists, and then she went into this classroom where the teacher said very simply to tell a story about herself.

"So I went home and took out a pen and told a story."

I am not going to tell you she now has a book on the bestseller list. She doesn't have a book at all. But what she has are memories that she calls up so beautifully they come alive.

Memories don't just remind you of when you were younger. That is obvious. In some mysterious way, when you go back to tell a story about that memory, you are there, and you are who you were then.

"We went to Lost Lagoon to see the new fountain," she wrote. "We were seated on blankets on the grass. As darkness fell there was a hush, followed by a burst of cheers as the night came alive with a shower of amazing colours from the fountain in the middle of the lagoon."

She is not being fancy. She is just remembering and writing her memory for others to see and feel.

"Sundays were family days. Many boarded the streetcars with picnic baskets and went off to Stanley Park. Many brought spaghetti and wieners or stew. The smells were wonderful and the sounds of laughter and children playing were beautiful."

Rosemary has a stack of stories. Some get read at her writing club. Some I read. But the only thing that really matters is that when she writes, she is not almost ninety. She is almost nine again.

And that is an ageless story.

Pain in the Head

The Last Word You Say Should Be the First You Think Of

I t should be easy. It looks easy. It sounds easy.

The last words in the story. They make a point and make you smile or raise your eyebrows or something, anything, just please have a reaction because this is what it has all built up to.

Please, dear editor, tell me what to say. (That is me in desperation.)

To think an editor only puts pictures together and then goes on to the next assignment is, well, wrong. The editors save me, every day.

I was at the Ancient and Honourable Hyack Anvil Battery watching men in red jackets put gun powder between massive steel anvils and then light it with red-hot pokers.

The story—if by any chance you don't know, and how could that be possible?—is more than a century old. It began when the bigwigs in Victoria said no other town could salute Queen Victoria. Only they could do it, which is a very stingy thing to say.

They wanted the honour all for themselves, and they went so far as to confiscate the one and only cannon in New Westminster, where it had been used by the city to salute their queen.

The folks in New West—which had been the capital until it was stolen from them through dirty politics—were mightily ticked off.

And it just so happened that the mayor of New West was also a blacksmith. And blacksmiths had anvils. And blacksmiths were not to be denied honouring their queen.

So the mayor got together some friends, and in the middle of Columbia Street, the main thoroughfare, they put one anvil down on the ground, put some gunpowder on it, put another anvil on top and touched it with a red-hot poker.

Boom! Or more accurately, bang! In either case, it was as loud as a cannon.

They did this twenty-one times for the twenty-one-anvil salute. I am sure the queen heard about it on the next ship that sailed, which would have been a couple of months later.

The bigwigs in Victoria heard about it a day later after a boat crossed the strait and someone ran to the capital shouting, "Do you know what those hooligans in the no-longer-capital city, which is not a *real* city, did?"

It was an act of total civil disobedience, one of the best ever, that did not cause anyone to get hurt but made a point: Don't Mess With New West.

And they kept on firing those anvils every year, except the one in which Queen Victoria died.

I love it so much that I have done the story consistently for twenty years on television.

A good story about independence should be repeated. It might spread the idea.

The men who fire the anvils all wear the red tunics that the original Royal Engineers wore as uniforms. They look classy, and they take the annual firing seriously, almost, mostly … Okay, not entirely.

As in every army, they have technical specialities: sniper, bombardier, tank driver. Except in the Hyack Anvil Battery. And please, let's stop a moment.

Hyack is a corruption of a Chinook word meaning "hurry up." The First Nations people lived there first, so it was only fitting they get the first word. Plus, it not only sounds good, but it makes everyone who comes into town ask, "What does *Hyack* mean?" And there starts a conversation and maybe a new friendship. Half the events in New West have *Hyack* in their names.

And I hate to explain because I know I don't have to but *battery* does not only mean something you put into a flashlight. *Battuere* is a Latin verb meaning "to beat." And that is exactly what cannons and other large guns are supposed to do.

Hence, a long time ago before there were flashlights *battuere* became *battery*, something that beats down anything standing in front of it, and those firing the cannons were in the battery. And a true artillery battery has numerous cannons because many cannons, naturally, do more beating down than just one cannon.

How it got into a flashlight is a bit of a stretch. But Benjamin Franklin, who helped found a country, started a post office, wrote political and philosophical pamphlets and spoke French fluently, also played with electricity. He put together a row of Leyden jars and found they had more zing than just one. A Leyden jar is a glass container with pieces of metal inside which can hold a small spark of electricity, about the same as what you get by running a comb through your hair. They were used by people experimenting with this ancient, exciting power. When Franklin discovered that numerous jars could deliver a big kick, he called them a battery, just like a row of cannons. Hence cannons became the powerhouses that we use in flashlights.

Words have strange ancestors, just as we do.

Anyway, the men in the red jackets firing the anvils have specialities, which they are proud of:

Those who lift up the anvil after it has fired are the lifter uppers. And there is a left-hand lifter upper and a right-hand lifter upper because if they got those positions mixed up the anvil might fall on a toe and that would hurt.

There is the swabber off-er, who takes a wet brush from a bucket of water and wipes off the embers of the gun powder from the bottom anvil before someone else puts more gun powder onto it. You instinctively know the value he has to the group.

And there is the putter on-er, who puts the gun powder on the anvil with a playing card on top. They use an eighth of a pound of gun powder. The Nine O'Clock Gun uses a quarter pound. The naval ships of wood with the iron cannons used a half pound. They were good for blowing holes in other ships, and for removing arms and legs.

The Hyack Anvil Battery explodes with peaceable blasts. And there is another tradition. When the first shot is fired the master of ceremonies, Archie Miller, who has been in charge almost as long as the battery has been firing, says, "And there go the ancient and honourable car alarms." The parking lot sounds like a preschool when nap time is needed.

But this year there was one new thing at this unwavering tradition, a lemonade stand. They did not have lemonade stands a hundred plus years ago. They had beer. And the original fire off-ers sometimes had too much beer, and some probably missed with the hot poker and some had trouble lifting the anvil back up. But they did have fun and the queen would have been amused.

We are very genteel in our traditions now. Five kids selling lemonade. "Who made it?" I asked.

"Our mother," said one who was about *this* big, no, smaller than that, a little smaller. Yes. You have it now.

"Why didn't you make it?"

Small One had the best comment of the day. "We don't know how to."

Blessings on the beauty of truth, honesty and kids. One small, smiling face not trying to be like a politician. Truth. The tradition is wonderful, but this kid was the best thing of the day and not one anvil was yet fired off.

His mother made the lemonade. Come on. Stand with me and think nothing is more touching than this moment. This is the moment I live for every day.

We finished the story. We got the firing. We got the selling of lem-onade. We were back in the edit room and I was happy. I had something fun, uplifting and different.

The editor, Gerald Christenson, put together the pictures as an editor does. Close-ups, followed by medium shots, then wide shots. It is actually much more artistic than that. The way I have described it is like saying an artist just puts small strokes next to medium. Not so.

Editors are artists.

And then we came to the lemonade kids.

"We have to put them in the story," I said.

Gerald looked at me with an eyebrow that did not quite rise, but almost.

"Of course," he said, trying to pretend as though he did not hear me saying we have to do what is obvious to anyone on the planet.

So he squeezed in a picture of the kids pouring the drink. Then he added the sound of me asking who made it. Then he put in the picture of the kid saying his mother did it.

Wonderful.

"So what do I say over the kids pouring?" I asked.

This is the great transition between gun powder and lemons.

What do I say? How do I say something in three seconds that makes sense and has meaning and fits in with the story?

What *do* I say?

Easy question. Hard answer. I try, "And away from the field is lemonade."

Gerald looks at me in a way that would have him sent to bed without dinner if this were a family. But this is not.

"You don't like that?"

Gerald looks again, the same way he looked earlier.

I try, "Something wet with the dry gun powder in the air."

The same look.

"Okay, help me."

In the old days, before I could put the words down with a microphone as we went along in the edit room, there was my typewriter. The one I told you about earlier.

I would write something. The editor would say no. I would write something else. Editor: No! Write something else. Editor: Better.

Write something else.

On a typical story the last line would be written ten times. Wait, who am I kidding? It would take up three sheets of paper and be fifteen or twenty lines long, all saying the same thing just a little differently. And then the editor would nod.

Editor: Okay. Thank you.

That is why I love editors.

Gerald, who has white hair and knows the way of the world, has simply saved me when my world was coming to an end, again.

Back to the anvil. I last said something about wet lemonade and dry gun powder. It was stupid.

"Okay, help me."

And that is when Gerald said, "Try something with tradition. That's what this is all about, right?"

Well, duh. I could have figured that out, in a week or two.

So I try, "And away from the gun powder, a new tradition."

It seems so simple. It seems so obvious. It is what editors do.

The story worked fine, with its new tradition.

This happens every day.

Wrong

It Sounds So Simple, It Must Be Easy

Living, storytelling, editing, it is all a work in progress. And just like with shoelaces, you need all the help you can get.

Now I am in a room with editor Kim Cirillo, working on another story. I told you about Kim in the story about the couple who met in a seniors' home and fell in love. She has a four-year-old, Micky, whose pictures are here and there and over there on a wall of her edit room.

My desperate searching is for a word, a thought, anything. Kim says, "Micky would say 'that's a really pretty flower.'"

Why didn't I think of that? Why didn't I think that what we are looking at is simply pretty, rather than trying to tie it in with the economy of the world or local politics? Why? Because I am like all of us. I try to make something sound important when it is simply really pretty.

But think like a child, with simplicity. Micky is right. We take the words of a four-year-old who is not there and it turns out just right. Thank you, Micky, even if you were not in the room, you saved the story.

Most editors I have worked with are like that. They fix the small things, then the big stuff repairs itself.

Vinh Nguyen is another editor. After almost half the things I say into the microphone he shakes his head. No.

"What do you mean, 'No'?"

"You could say it better."

"But that's the best I have."

"No it's not. Try it with a word about the ..." (whatever the story is about).

And I do. And he nods. And I am happy.

Then he is on the phone with someone, speaking Vietnamese. He is fluent. Of course he is—it is his first language. His father was one of the boat people. If you don't know what that is, look it up on Google.

It was terrible, it was hard and it was done to save families. Vinh is from one of those families. If he says something is not strong enough, it is not strong enough.

He has a new son, Owen, who he says is learning to jump but he just throws up his arms and the top of his body. The legs have not yet learned to follow.

I think this is the neatest thing in the world and I would love to do a story about it. What Owen is doing is the pure joy of learning something while still not knowing what he has learned.

Then I am with Michelle Scott. Same thing. I ask her what I should say about a picture. She smiles and says that's *my* job.

I say I need help. Michelle knows about helping. We all have personal things in our lives, some more than others. Michelle knows more than others. That makes her the best writer in the station, even if she has never written a word.

Then she says, "Keep it simple" and I do. Sometimes simple words have deep roots.

And there is Jeannine Avelino who runs marathons on roadways and cross country races over mountains. It is crazy if you can run twenty-six miles and pretty much the same thing through the woods, and I salute you. But she has done this so many times that she can't count the number. She has been through pain and determination and she has gotten to the finish line. She has done things I could not begin to think of. I'll listen to anything she says.

And Adam Lee, who loves the Blue Jays. If there is a baseball analogy about missing a pitch or stealing a base, he has it. So I write according to his signals. He is the catcher, telling me no, that is not the right pitch. And then yes, a curve now would be the winner, we hope.

So I throw a curve. And he says no. "Didn't curve fast enough. Try again."

I do, and he smiles.

That is the way a story is written.

There are other editors: Carl Wayman, who lives in a dark world, which means he turns the lights off in his edit room. The only glow is from the monitors, displaying the subject of whatever he is dealing with. Scary. But on the other hand, he is doing what every school and career coach suggests: concentrating.

His stories come out of the dark full of light and life.

And there is James Buck, the boss, the chief editor. He has a painting of a three-masted sailing ship on his wall. It came from his grandmother in Germany. His grandfather was a carpenter on one of those ships.

The ship's carpenter was the one who fixed things when they needed fixing so that the ship could keep sailing. His grandfather was, in short, the ship's editor, except he carved emergency wood out of hunks of oak that were as hard as steel. And he made repairs that no one figured could be done and he did it while the ship was in a storm and the swells were rocking it back and forth, and the work had to be done or terrible things would happen—sort of like a newsroom at deadline.

The ship is on the wall while James is working, and the deadline is an approaching storm. He is the editing carpenter, saving a story from sinking.

Carpenter, editor, artist, coach, counsellor, paramedic. All the same.

Sabrina Gans also tells me what to say. I have a lot of tellers for my little sayings. Sabrina has two small children, Emily and Reese. She reads to her kids every night, which is wonderful. That is how you make readers, and readers grow up to change the world.

One thing she reads to them is Shel Silverstein.

"Who?" I asked.

"You don't know?" That would be with the surprised tone, and *how could you not know?* implied.

"No."

She is thinking deprived childhood.

She brings me books by Shel Silverstein. This is the kind of writing I love! It is short.

He writes poems that are not poems. Or at least he wrote them until he left this planet for other adventures. And he was famous, though I did not know that.

So I read and read Shel Silverstein and wrote some poems that are not poems. Short ones, like him. And sent them to the publisher. And he said … Well, you know what he said. Read the introduction to this book.

And it was because of Sabrina, and her kids who she reads to, that this book exists.

That is the power of an editor.

And, Sabrina, don't worry, your daughter will get the slime out of her hair, and your son will hit a home run.

The slime happened while we were working on another story. Sabrina got a phone call from her husband. Their daughter had slime in her hair. What can he do?! What should he do?! Should he cut off her hair?!

"Wash it," she said.

Then she added, "Men!"

And we went back to editing the television story of the day.

The Sign Master

The Best Writers Know About Pain,
but Don't Write About It

To half the people in North Vancouver, Bob Gibson's writing is what saves them from a bad day. The other half don't know about him, at least not yet.

Bob writes one page at a time, no more than five lines long and usually ten words or less, depending on how long the words are.

His writing:

I COULD BE A
MORNING PERSON
IF MORNINGS HAPPENED
AROUND NOON.

And:

WENT TO BUY
CAMOUFLAGE
GEAR ...
COULDN'T FIND ANY.

And:

ONE DAY CANADA
WILL TAKE OVER
THE WORLD.

THEN YOU'LL BE SORRY

The words are on a sign outside his printing shop on Forbes Avenue in North Vancouver. Anyone coming on or off Esplanade sees it.

If you are going too fast, you have to slow down or you won't finish reading before you finish passing it. And no, he is not distracting drivers. There have been no accidents because of his signs. But there have been a lot of people not speeding.

TONIGHT'S

PROCRASTINATION

WORKSHOP

POSTPONED

The word *procrastination* took up the entire line in the sign.

"I steal the ideas," Bob said.

No, he really does not. He borrows them and enhances them and shares them and makes many smile with them. That is not stealing.

"And I get a lot from my wife's cousin," he said.

The way he said it I knew he wanted to give someone else credit, and that is a very kind thing to do.

AUTOCORRECT

HAS BECOME

MY WORST

ENEMA

I saw that and thought, "I have a long way to go as a writer."

Bob said the original sign outside his shop had been there for years, decades, and no one read it. And that's because it said "Printing." And then it said how many copies for how much money.

All signs say that, or they say "Haircuts for ten dollars." No, wait, no sign says that now. "Haircuts for thirty dollars." Cheap. But no one reads those either.

The name of his shop is Contact Printing, and just for a lark one day he put together some letters that said:

PRINTING
IS NOT A
CONTACT SPORT.

Bob does not remember why he did it, he just did. And he felt good.

He and his staff climb a ladder to put up the letters by hand—no computer—and each letter is at least ten years old. When the black paint wears off they fill it in with felt pens.

Within minutes of "PRINTING IS NOT A CONTACT SPORT" they were getting phone calls. Not bad. In fact, pretty good. One of those bright ideas.

He does not know if business increased, but I bet it did.

And that was just the beginning.

DOES REFUSING
TO GO TO THE GYM
COUNT AS
RESISTANCE TRAINING

And:

I'M HAVING AN
OUT OF MONEY
EXPERIENCE

Bob took out a paper file folder, the kind no one under thirty has ever seen.

It is like the icon on your computer that says "folder," except this was a real folder, made of heavy paper and filled with papers. The only difference between Bob's and the computer's folder is he held it in his hand and it felt good, a feeling you don't get with a computer folder.

Inside the folder were hundreds of notes, all of his signs or attempts at signs with *X*s marked through some of them. That is the way a writer works.

You get an idea, then you put an *X* through it. Why? Because it is a dumb idea. You get another idea. You feel good. Then you put an *X* through it because it is worse than dumb.

More ideas. More *X*s. And then something works.

It is sort of like Thomas Edison thinking, "An automatic fly swatter? *X*. A reusable rat trap? *X*. A lightbulb? Just might be something people could use."

One of Bob's that did not get an *X*:

THE FUTURE IS

NOT WHAT IT

USED TO BE

That is my favourite.

Then we asked if he could show us how he writes. No pressure. We are just standing there with a camera that is recording. Again, no pressure.

He gets a phone call. He makes notes on what the person on the phone is saying. He says goodbye. Then he looks at us as though we are just another couple of customers and he is going to give us what we want. He writes on the corner of a sheet of paper:

THE CREATIVE SIGN

IS ON THE

OTHER SIDE

That is not very good, I think.

Then he says, "I'll write that on both sides."

Brilliant, and funny, and it is a punchline that drivers will not get until the afternoon when they are going the other way.

I am so happy. And Bob is happy.

When we left I mentioned to the cameraman that it is so good to be around someone who is cheerful. He makes the day better.

After the story was on the air a friend of mine said he knew Bob. He asked if I knew that Bob's son was killed in a traffic accident a few years ago. Both his son and his son's girlfriend died.

Bob never mentioned that. He never alluded to it. He never looked sad. He never did or said anything that would make me ask if there was something else he wanted to mention.

He just writes happy notes that make drivers smile.

In his short pages of poetry, he has written an epic story of dealing with pain and heartbreak, without ever mentioning the pain and heartbreak.

Impressing the Intern

A Long Story Ending with a Lesson in Humility

They don't get paid. They are excited and open to learning and hoping to get something out of it.

They are the interns.

I am asked if I would mind if one of them rode around with the cameraman and me on this semi-rainy, semi-sunny day.

Of course not. It is fun to share the excitement of looking for something you don't know is there, then finding it, then turning it into something hopefully entertaining and possibly somewhat meaningful, all in a couple of hours.

I tell everyone that anyone can do it. I tell anyone who wants to be a reporter they can do it.

Maddie Doyle is introduced to me. She looks like many second-year students in college or university. And, in some ways, she looks like others of her generation: a coffee cup in one hand and a cellphone in the other and texting with one hand while walking with friends, who are also texting. In another way she is different. She wants to be a reporter. Hence, she can do no wrong.

I am looking forward to taking along Maddie, who will learn how news can be done in a way they don't teach in school.

We get in an suv in a back alley. Steve Murray is the cameraman. He is a trendy, downtown kind of guy who lives in a condo just above a fire station, so he has never, since I have known him, gotten a full night of sleep.

Also, the people who live above him don't have carpeting and appear to be studying flamenco dancing.

According to all the studies I have read, Steve should not be conscious or sane.

But he is a good cameraman. Camera operators are a rare breed, kind of like the Marines of the news business. They do the grunt work. They are there first. Sometimes they are there alone.

They have to be there. That is the one and only rule, besides knowing how to work the camera and having a good eye for composition and understanding how to deal with different light levels and knowing how to string microphones across a crowded floor and knowing how to send pictures across the city or province and knowing how to carry not only the camera but often a tripod which is heavier than the camera and hauling a bag of replacement parts and batteries and wires and knowing how at a big-time press conference to squeeze between other camera operators who have staked out spots and will not let you in and you have to threaten, then beg, then hope, to get a spot to keep your job, and knowing how, in a moment of panic when you just *have* to get that shot, to not push the record button twice, which is a human impulse to push and push, except that means that the camera is not recording and you don't realize it and all of those irreplaceable, amazing things that happened in front of you that were going to win you a Pulitzer or at least a thank you from the boss are not there, darn—but most of all you have to be there.

The best cameraman I have ever known, who has earned a fortune off his photography and opened a small hospital in Africa because he took so many pictures there and has had a cover on *National Geographic*, is often asked the secret behind his work.

"F/16 and be there."

His name is Grant Faint. You can look him up on Google and be amazed. He is from East Vancouver and now lives in a home overlooking the world on Vancouver Island.

He is, honest to heaven, an inspiration. When we worked together in news he would stop and take pictures of mountains and clouds, then get back to the news.

Sorry, I know I have told you this before, but a second lesson is always good so that you know you can do it too, if you believe you can. Grant was unknown. He sent his pictures unsolicited to an agency in New York, who rejected them like most unsolicited pictures and stories.

Then one day he pulled over in front of a newsstand and said, "Come with me."

He picked out a national US magazine and opened to a giant, full-page ad for a cigarette. The background showed the North Shore mountains.

"That's my picture," he said.

He made more off that ad than he would in a week of work, chasing cops and criminals.

The only thing that needs explaining is f/16. He began work in film when you could not just keep recording and later pick out what you liked. Film was expensive. And f/16 is a setting on a camera that lets in a certain amount of light.

Some camera people I work with now do not know this. They are young, and despite that are good photographers. But as for f-stops, the camera does it all.

If you had to set your camera before each shot and keep an eye on the amount of film you used, you would learn to set up your shots very carefully.

Grant did. But again, the most important thing for a still photographer or a video news gathering person is: Be there.

That is something we don't have to worry about on this day with Maddie, because I'm hoping she sees how to find and report on the oddball stories that keep the world going.

I thought maybe I could teach her some reporting shortcuts. She had already been out with four other reporters and cameras and I knew they had gone straight to their assignments and done their work.

This would be different.

The hard thing was that the day before I had tripped while running to catch a bus and banged my knee, and it was stiff, so it was hard to get in and out of the truck. Very hard.

We drove, and saw nothing. We drove some more and I joked to Maddie that as soon as any of us see anything then she can watch Steve do his magic.

We saw nothing. We went to a park, because parks always have *something*. Steve carried his camera. I limped. We saw nothing.

Maddie asked if she could carry Steve's camera. I said that is good training because reporters who help camera operators are very kind and very, very smart, because it is smart to be kind to everyone but especially to those you rely on for your income.

She said it was heavy. He said it had a wide-angle lens that made it heavier than the others.

We got back in Steve's truck and continued to fail in finding something to show Maddie how easy it is to do this.

Then Steve said he remembered meeting a woman at the Salvation Army Harbour Light Detox Centre at Easter who wore bunny ears while serving meals.

He had heard that she also sang and cut hair, which she was not doing that day. Maybe she would still be there.

I was feeling very thankful to Steve, but seriously disappointed that I had not spotted anything that looked like nothing but turned out to be something wonderful. That would be the thing Maddie would take back to school and into her reporting career: If you as a reporter keep looking, you can find something significant in almost anything.

That was my wish, but it was not coming true.

Steve went into the detox centre and came out with Christina. Bless him. Christina had been an addict for twenty years. She had lost everything. But she had now been clean for nine years. She was finding everything again. She was happy.

There was no haircutting that day, but sure, she would sing—and she did a beautiful version of "I Can See Clearly Now." She was standing in front of the centre. Behind her were people laughing and pushing each other, joking, smoking, the usual sight on this street.

Christina sang about seeing obstacles in her way.

Before she got clean, she had tried to kill herself.

She sang about it now being a day filled with sunshine.

Leaning against the wall of the building was a man who started to sing with her. His name was Giles. He had been clean for one week.

Christina stepped near him and together they sang again. It was truly a bright and sun-filled day.

"Is it really?" I asked.

"You bet."

"Yes, you bet it is," said Giles.

What a perfect story! I thanked Steve. The only thing was Maddie had not learned anything from me. The result of all my years of training and doing: zero.

"Sometimes the camera people do all the work," I said to her.

She smiled, a very big smile, and said, "I know. That's why I want to work with cameras."

"What?" I asked, sort of quietly.

"I don't want to be a reporter. I came out to watch Steve." She did not add, "Not you."

She said she was not taking the journalism course in school. She was in the television department, which teaches everything except reporting.

One other thing I forgot to mention that is important in this career, and every other one: humility. They don't teach that in school either.

A Camera at Work

Something Comes from Nothing, Sometimes

I t was wonderful. Super. The best, super best.

An open umbrella ripping down the street between rows of parked cars.

It was a windy day, the rain had stopped, and I guess somewhere not too far away from us an umbrella had broken free, and now it was dancing over the asphalt.

What else could anyone hope for? What could be easier? A few minutes of watching and a day counted as work. Please don't get jealous or angry. It's what I do.

I think of the image of untethered joy, of acrobatic tumbling and twirling and bouncing off colourful walls of steel and changing directions. It is all too good to imagine.

I get out of the truck. Steve Hughes gets out too. I am praying his camera comes out like the wind.

But the back door must be opened and a lock must be undone to release a metal drawer and a lock on a safeguard inside the drawer must be unlocked before the camera is free. That's a lot of locks.

And the wind is dying. I see the umbrella slow, then stop as Steve starts his camera.

Darn. But there is the overriding philosophical belief that good things happen when you wish hard enough.

I wish. No wind. Wish harder. Still no wind.

Quit? And look for something else? No, we can't do that. Did you see how good it looked when it was looking good?

Well, it was.

Remember: Never give up. Okay, that is a fairly trite thing to say when you are waiting for an umbrella to move. So I didn't say it. But it did look good. And I did say, "Let's just wait a bit."

Steve has been shooting news for thirty years.

He was at Mount St. Helens recording fire and ash. He said he was scared.

Today, an umbrella.

He was in New Orleans after Hurricane Katrina. Frightening, troubling pictures.

Today, an umbrella.

He was threatened at gunpoint while shooting a crime story.

Today, well, you know what today is, an exercise in patience waiting for the inorganic to pretend in our eyes that it has organic, movable life.

Then the wind comes again. A big wind. Steve gets video of the umbrella blowing across the street, then rolling, then crossing the street again and I know this is almost enough to show on television. Almost, but not quite enough.

And that extra bit we need is coming now, with the wind picking up and we will have an exciting, offbeat story—after all, how many times on national or local television have you seen an entire story of an umbrella blowing down the street?—and we almost have it, until the umbrella jumps between two parked cars and gets stuck.

Umbrella, how can you do this to me?! I want to give you fame and put you on television. And who doesn't want to be on TV? How many of your fellow brollies who came off the umbrella assembly line can say they have been on TV?

Okay, in Vancouver most of them have. That happens during any street scene from September to April. You have me on that one. Oh, you have been on TV already? Several times. Okay, but how many of your fellow bumbershoots—sorry, you did not know you are a bumbershoot?—have been on TV when it was *not* raining?

Bumbershoot, by the way, is a portmanteau—a fancy word made by putting two words together—that was used in the nineteenth century, combining *umbrella* and *parachute*. So there, Mr. Umbrella, you learned something.

But the umbrella is now trapped and we can't leave it there. I know that may sound silly, okay, even worse than silly. But just imagine if you saw someone leave something trapped and not try to help!

Again, I know we are talking about an umbrella, but in the universe of things you can't do—you cannot leave it there.

But we cannot interfere with it because that is not what we do. We record reality, we do not change it for our sake. This is a very important and serious rule.

I will not allow even a leaf to be moved to make a better shot, because if someone sees us doing that, they can rightfully say we are altering the news. If we do it with a leaf, what is to stop us from doing it with everything? Nothing. So, no interfering.

This of course does not count when someone is actually in trouble or has a problem. Yes, we help. But as for anything less than imminent death or disaster, hands off.

(There was one exception. You can read about it later, in the chapter about daffodils, and make up your own mind.)

We wait for the wind to blow the umbrella free. It is not going to happen.

A man walks down the street, looks at us looking at the umbrella, then looks at the umbrella and asks, "Is that yours?"

"No, is it yours?" we ask, hopefully.

"No. But why are you staring at it?"

"We're waiting for it to move."

He looks perplexed. "Then why don't you just move it?"

"We're waiting for the wind to move it."

He shakes his head, steps off the sidewalk and picks up the umbrella and starts handing it to us before I can shout, "No!"

"You don't want it?" he asks. He is just being kind, he thinks.

"No, we were just waiting for the wind."

He folds up the umbrella and puts it down near someone's front steps and leaves, knowing there are some things about life he does not understand.

And that is perfect. The umbrella was saved by someone, not quite a heroic act but at least something happened which is better than nothing happened, which is what happens too often. The world was changed in the smallest, tiniest way.

Over a picture of the umbrella we told the owner where it was, just in case: Manitoba Street and Thirty-Seventh Avenue.

And we had a story you just don't find in many places. Some of you may be saying, "Thank goodness." Some may be saying, "We need more umbrellas on television."

Some who I work with said, quietly, "Is that all he does, show a picture of an umbrella going down the street?"

Basically, yes. But it took a lifetime to get there.

My Education

You Can Learn by Watching

The reporting process is simple, as you know. I do nothing. I carry almost nothing. I worry about nothing. I rely on seeing something wonderful and ask my companion on the voyage of discovery to take some pictures.

Or to be more truthful, when my eyes get heavy and I doze off because we have not seen anything exciting for, well, forever, the camera operator shouts, "How about that?" and I wake up and we begin a story.

When I was a copy boy in New York, young hopeful journalists did not go to school to learn journalism. First of all, you never used the word *journalist*. That was too pretentious. You wanted to be a reporter, plain and simple. You got a job as a copy boy or girl, and you sat on a hard wooden bench waiting to hear "Copy!" And you would jump and grab the paper coming out of a manual typewriter and carry it to the city desk.

And there you would watch an old man smoking a cigarette read the paper, make a few changes, and then yell, "Copy!" But you were standing right there.

And you would carry the paper to the news desk where an old man smoking a cigar would squint, then take a pencil to a paper rendition of a newspaper page and draw a line across the top of three columns, which meant it was a major story, and yell, "Copy!"

But of course you were standing next to him and you would carry the paper to the copy desk which was shaped like a horseshoe and had the chief copy editor in the middle and the copy readers on the rim and you would give the paper to the chief and he would give it to one of the people on the outside and they would read and make magical changes.

These were the brilliant people. I met one who was listed in *Who's Who in America.* That was a major book on the most influential people in the country. One of them was sitting on the rim of the copy desk where I was delivering pieces of paper.

A good editor does not change things. A good editor improves things. They were good editors.

In half a minute, a word was altered and a punctuation mark was added. The rapid-fire news story was taking shape.

Then these copy editors had to write the headline that went over the story. That was creative-genius writing.

Two things sold this newspaper: pictures and headlines. Followed by captions, and after that the written stories.

Of course, the story was the impetus for the pictures and headlines, which means the story was the soul. The pictures and words were the muscle that delivered the opening punches of the story.

Headlines were hard to write. They had to be both concise and pithy. The first line had to end with a verb:

Mobster Killed

The second line had to tell the story in a juicy way:

Girlfriend Sought

But the second line had to be the same physical length as the first line, which the above example is not.

But this is:

Mobster Killed,

Sweetie Sought

And the copy editors had to do this while the minute hand on the clock above the desk is going around once, twice, don't let it go three times. Okay, I have it.

Try that all night long without screaming, which sometimes happened.

And what was the incentive?

The best headline of the week was awarded three days' pay. And the second-best two days' pay. And the third-best a day's pay.

This was better than school.

I figure I learned almost everything I ever knew as a copy boy. I had to sharpen pencils, change typewriter ribbons between one story being finished and another begun, which was impossible. But necessary.

I followed around reporters and watched them gather facts, and got whatever information they asked me to get, and I followed photographers and watched them sometimes risk their future to get a picture. Then I ran like crazy to get their film back to the newsroom.

Again, no journalism school. The only way was to work your way up as a copy runner, and the top one, by seniority, would eventually be offered a chance to be an editor, reporter or photographer, starting at the bottom. You chose.

I did not want to be an editor because I could not come up with those headlines. And I saw all the equipment that photographers had to carry and thought, "I know I would lose some of it."

Reporters only had to have a pencil and a few scraps of paper to write some names.

I became the bottom reporter, and left the hard work to others.

A West Coast Story

Just Because You Get the Opportunity
You Don't Have to Get Even

H e was an up-and-coming store clerk. He was white.
　　　She was a girl of mixed race. Her father was white, her
mother Cree.

But the white boy and the girl of mixed race were in love. Sort of
Romeo and Juliet.

Her father said okay, partly because the white boy was big.

He was way over six foot when most men were five and a half
feet tall, and more than two hundred pounds when most men were
under 150.

She was small. Five foot two. Tiny. He could protect her.

They married.

He worked his way up, but one night he said something wrong to
a First Nations chief and the chief's people tried to kill him.

She stood up to them. The tiny girl threw blankets and pots and
pans at their feet and said, "Take these. Leave him alone. He's just a
dumb white man."

Or something like that. And it worked.

He got promoted and moved to the high-class neighbourhood in
the high-class city of Victoria, where he ran the shop.

She was shunned. Ostracized. Ignored.

The Victorian ladies said no. No visits, no talk, no tea and crumpets.
She's not white. Her name was Amelia. Her husband was James.

That is, James Douglas. To you and me, Sir James Douglas, the
George Washington of British Columbia. Forgive me for that awkward

comparison. George was the father of America, and James was the father of British Columbia. George got the English out of America and James kept the Americans from absorbing BC into their country. Before James was the father of this province, he was its protector.

He got Queen Victoria to claim the land as a colony, just in the nick of time before America would make it theirs.

He was knighted by the queen which made Amelia become Lady Amelia.

Which meant the women of Victoria had to visit, and curtsy before her. They did, because they had to. She gave them tea in her drawing room. They talked about the weather.

She never condemned them. She never criticized. She never reminded them of what they had done. She never hurt them.

She was gracious.

She was tiny. She was of mixed race. She was a lady, and there was no better woman to have as the first First Lady of this province.

Prejudice

The Only Way to Experience Something Is to Experience It

I haven't written about this before. It is very personal, but on the other hand, it is important.

You know the black guy you saw someone move away from on the bus, or the Chinese family your neighbours hope does not move in next door, or the man who wears a turban who wants a job but human resources wonders if he can really handle it?

I know you are not a prejudiced schmuck. You are a good person. I believe that.

But you know others who worry if someone different comes too close. I know you do.

Let me tell you a story about a friend of mine. I met him when I was in the US Air Force. When you are in the military, any branch, it is not just part of your life, it *is* your life.

It demands total obedience and loyalty. That is the only way to get a group of ordinary people to go out and kill other people while knowing that the chances of them being killed is almost a sure bet.

In the air force there was a fellow who needed extra money because he was married and had a small child. They lived off the air base in a tiny cottage.

"Cottage" sounds nice. It was tiny. It had a tin roof which sucked in the heat and did not stop the cold. They barely scraped by.

This fellow tried to earn money by writing for magazines and newspapers, which paid very little, but it was something.

The base he was assigned to was in the deep south. His wife was of mixed ancestry. It was difficult to survive there. In the town there were separate water fountains for "coloured" and "white" and they were labelled as such. There were separate entrances to the movie house for the same.

The cafeteria on the air base was the only place in the county where a black airman and a white airman who had spent the morning loading rockets onto an interceptor jet could have coffee together. It was illegal in the town right next to the base.

This friend of mine heard of a tiny circus that was coming to town. It had one baby elephant and one ringmaster who pretended one small elephant made a circus. My friend went to it and took pictures and wrote a story about it.

He developed the pictures in the bathroom of his tiny cottage. It was at night when it was dark and no one would use the bathroom.

He wrote the story very carefully, the best he could. And the city editor bought it and said it was pretty good.

Then he waited to be paid. And he waited and waited. And waited some more.

When he was off work on the air base he went to the newspaper and saw the publisher. He was sitting in a big wooden swivel chair with his feet on the desk. He was smoking a cigar.

"What do you want?" asked the publisher.

"I just want to know if I can get paid for that circus story?"

The publisher reached alongside his legs and picked up a cheque that was on his desk.

"You want this?" he asked.

"Yes, sir."

And this is what my friend told me the publisher said.

"We don't like people like you. We don't like them at all."

"Could I get paid?" my friend asked.

"Paid? You want to be paid?"

"Yes, sir."

"I told you we don't like people like you."

"Yes, sir. But could I get paid for that story?"

The publisher sat for a long while. My friend does not remember how long, but it was long.

Then the publisher said, "Here, you can get paid." And he reached over past the edge of his desk and dropped the cheque on the floor.

My friend told me he wanted to walk out. He wanted to show some dignity and strength. But he needed the money.

So he bent down and picked the cheque up off the floor.

"Don't you ever come back here," the publisher told my friend.

The cheque was for twenty-five dollars. It bought a week's groceries.

My friend went on to write other articles for magazines and other newspapers and did okay. But he told me never to let myself hurt someone because of how they look or who they talk to or who they marry.

That was the most important story he ever wrote, and this is the first time he will see it in print.

Harmonica Man

You Can Survive Anything, if You Decide to Survive It

H ere's how to live well, without bitterness, even though no one
would have blamed you for being bitter.

Harry Aoki was born in Canada, and when he was twenty-one years
old the police came for him. It was just after December 7, 1941, a day
that changed the world, and Harry's life.

On that day, Japan bombed the US Navy base at Pearl Harbor in
Hawaii. Harry was Canadian but he looked Japanese. His parents were
Japanese. He knew almost nothing about Japan.

His parents had brought their children for a visit ten years earlier
but none of them understood anything. They did not speak Japanese.
They knew no customs. The girls did not wear kimonos.

Okay, they could handle chopsticks as well as forks. Who can't?

But what Harry did was play the violin. He was magnificent. Everyone
said he had a great future, probably with some big-name orchestra.

And then the police came.

"You have one hour to get everything that you want to take with you.
And you can only take one suitcase," they said.

His violin, his precious violin that he had played for ten years, the
violin that knew every stroke of his fingers, the violin that whispered
sweetness into his ears, was too big for the suitcase.

He walked out onto the street, ready to be loaded into a wagon and
taken away because he had committed the crime of looking Japanese,
then he turned and ran back.

Harry grabbed his harmonica.

They are beautiful instruments, but they are not violins. Harmonicas make sweet sounds, but at the level of a campfire singalong, not a concert hall.

Harry was sent to a sugar beet farm in Alberta. Like so many other Japanese Canadians who were interned, Harry thought if he obeyed the rules and caused no trouble he would be accepted back into society when the war was over and given back his possessions.

Wrong.

During the day, he took care of the endless fields. In the darkness of the night he played his harmonica.

Then he took a correspondence course with the University of Chicago in music theory. How do you write letters about sounds? But he did, and he was offered a scholarship, until the mention of where he was living came up.

No scholarship.

After the war his family did not get back their house. No one got back anything that they left behind.

Harry played his harmonica on small-town shows on the radio. He worked at whatever job he could get.

Some people heard him play. They told others. Then others told others.

Twenty years after he left the sugar beet fields he was on stage with the string ensemble of the Calgary Philharmonic Orchestra, playing Mozart—on his harmonica.

A few years later he was music director for the Commonwealth Games in Edmonton.

The notes from his harmonica went into ears of people of all colours and sounded equally beautiful.

He was never outwardly bitter about his treatment. He spent the rest of his life trying to bring races together through music. He died at ninety-one peacefully. Someone played a harmonica at his funeral.

The Pool Shark

When You Use What You Have You Don't Need Anything Else

H e applied for the job that he knew he was qualified for, and he did have good qualifications.

No job.

He applied for another one, same thing.

Lance Yip was an A student in trigonometry, A in geometry, A in physics and of course A in mathematics, which is the basis of all of those brain-numbing studies.

His high school counsellor told him he should nail a good job with no problem. But his high school counsellor knew what would really happen. He just did not want to destroy Lance's dreams. He would let the world outside of school do that.

Lance was Chinese, and this was the early 1960s and although you cannot believe it now when you look downtown at morning rush hour and see waves of Asian men and women with suits and briefcases and coffee cups and cellphones going into those black towers, there was a time not so long ago, when: "You're Chinese? Sorry."

No job. No, you cannot live in this neighbourhood. No, you cannot buy this house.

If you have not been there you cannot image how it hurts. And, beyond that, how bewildering it is. You know you can do the job. You can do it better than some who have it. But you can't get it.

So Lance went to the pool hall. He had friends there. It was not sleazy. It was not bad. It was a meeting place. And when Lance walked in, his friends groaned.

"Not again. Who's going to play Lance?" Then they laughed because no one could play Lance, not play him and win.

"Pool and billiards is geometry," he said. "It is also physics." And calculating the odds to bet who would win and how much you could take from someone without them getting ticked off was math and probability, which he was also good at.

So he went to work at the one job he could get. He signed up for an independent franchise of floating pool sharks. No application required.

"I had ten dollars. That's it, nothing else, when I seriously went to work with a cue stick."

The balls went into the pockets and the cash came across the table.

"Six months later I bought a house."

He would pick a new pool hall every few days and hang around, shooting just par or below. Then the betting would start. He would win a game. That meant a little cash in his pocket. Then another, and more cash.

"But don't get greedy," he said. "Just make it look like it was a lucky streak." If anyone suspected he was a shark he would get no games. He would be driven out of the building.

When the larger bets were there, "it was like playing chess," he said. "I would line up balls so the other guy could not get a shot."

That was control of the kind you see in those movies about famous pool hustlers. But in the movies they shoot the scene over and over until the ball stops where they want.

In Lance's case he coaxed, he did not jab, the blue chalked tip of the cue stick onto a white ball, which rolled across the green felt until it hit another ball, which rolled until it stopped just at the spot where it blocked his opponent's shot.

"I haven't had a job in thirty years," he said.

His biggest challenge was leaving a pool hall before he had milked it clean and dried up his income. His biggest accomplishment, finding new places to tap a ball into a far pocket and say, "My gosh, that was a lucky shot."

His job was physiological and mathematical. It was cunning and coyness and knowing when to lose and when to win.

He worried. He faked. He sometimes missed a shot that he knew he should have had and lost.

That happens. It was not easy. But he made it look easy.

When I met him in a recreation centre in North Burnaby, he was playing with friends.

"It is useless to go against him," one of them said.

Lance is no longer working. He has some money in the bank.

"Retirement is challenging," he said. "I can't sleep late and go to the pool hall in the afternoon. Now I'm up early and go to the park and get sunshine and fresh air. First time in my life."

But sometimes he plays, just for fun. Go to the Eileen Dailly Rec Centre in North Burnaby. Look for someone with receding hair and an honest face. Ask if he wants to shoot a game with you.

Learn humility.

And She Deserves It

The Tooth Fairy Has Raised Her Rates

S hawn Foss is a cameraman at CTV. He is of dark- and light-skinned mixed heritage. There are so many ways of mixing people. All of them result in something new and beautiful and at the same time something that people who fear new things scorn and fear. Life is a crazy experiment.

But this is not about cameras or race. It is about the Tooth Fairy, who, if you are four or five or six, might seem much more important than those other things.

Shawn and his wife wanted children, and none were coming. So they adopted one.

Shawn knows about adoption. He was adopted, and it was not easy. He had a label put on him before he knew what labels were, or before he knew what anything was.

He did not know he was "difficult to place." It was a good thing he could not read when he was six months old or his first bedtime story would have been *No One Wants Me* and that is not a good way to go to sleep. It is not nice what we sometimes do to children.

But someone, some two ones, did want him and they wanted him deeply and he took in all they gave and grew big and happy and those other mushy things.

Anyway, after he and his wife adopted a child, you know what happened. Of course it did. "You never know," someone said earlier, "but this often happens." They had two of their own. Twins. Then they had another.

In the olden days, whatever those were, four kids was nothing. Four kids was not enough to milk the cow and gather the eggs and do those other kid things that would now make kids say, "What are you talking about? Milk a what? Gather eggs? They come in cartons. And suppose the cow or chicken bit me? I'm calling Child Protection Services."

Shawn's kids would not do that. They are nice. They have nice parents.

But they are four. And not just four, but four all about the same age, which is a challenge, especially to the Tooth Fairy because they all started losing their teeth at the same time.

"Do you know how much the Tooth Fairy is giving now?" Shawn asked me while we were hunting for something to put on TV, like maybe a wandering Tooth Fairy.

"No. Back long ago my kids got fifty cents from her," I said.

"Are you kidding? Fifty cents would not trade for a filling that fell out," said Shawn. "Generally the going rate is now five dollars."

"Per tooth?!"

That is me, who has not been in contact with said fairy for, well, for a while.

And I calculate: four kids times five dollars, and each kid has a couple dozen teeth. That is not a scientific count. That is a guess. And some of those teeth don't come out until the Tooth Fairy says the kids are way past the age when they need the cash. But five times four times some big number comes out to be …

What?!

Come on. "How much is the Tooth Fairy costing you?" I asked.

Shawn smiled. "When you see them in the morning reaching under their pillow, it's worth it," he said.

The Tooth Fairy and I had a little talk after this, and the Tooth Fairy said, "I'm not in charge of budget."

"But five dollars is a bit much," I said.

"All I do is take the front ones, the back ones and the middle ones to a kind of tooth heaven where there is chocolate and lollipops and of course plenty of toothbrushes and floss. And I make sure they use them."

"But five dollars?"

"Do you see the faces of the children in the morning when they reach under their pillows?"

"But—" I started to say when she interrupted. "It doesn't matter who puts a tooth under a pillow, I take them all. None are 'difficult to place.'"

The Tooth Fairy really should be given a bigger job, like running the world.

You Never Know

Hang On for the Surprise Because

You never know. I learned that from a woman at Riverview Hospital who wore a hockey helmet because she was what they vividly called a "head banger."

Sad. But behind her head banging and her sometimes anguished face, she was beautiful. Her name was Ruth. We spent a lot of time together.

That was when I was doing stories about mental health, and the government was closing Riverview to save money, which turned out to be more important than saving minds and lives.

The theory was—you probably know this—but the theory was that drugs had been made that would control schizophrenia. That was the main illness at the hospital. So the patients were given the drugs and told they could live a good life if they simply took them, and then they were released into the world outside the hospital. There were no support services. None.

I did story after story showing that the government had no services in place, but it did not stop them from letting the patients leave Riverview and go downtown where there was … Let me look for the word … Nothing. No one to help them. No one to care for them. No one to remind them to take their medicine.

And as a result, many of the patients who were walking the streets instead of the halls of the hospital did not take the little pills. The drugs had side effects. They slowed your walk. They slowed your mind.

Or they just forgot to take them, like one forgets to take vitamins. And on the street, with no care, they quickly went for other drugs, the ones that made you feel good or forget.

And then they were forgotten. And that contributed to the homeless being thought of as having mental health problems. It is a terrible shame. Don't trust those in power. Some are good. Some are not.

Much more care is given now. There is hope. There is support. There is a way to have a good life if you have schizophrenia. But many are still wandering the streets.

If you know someone with schizophrenia you most likely say, "Oh, God, help this person." Not every experience of schizophrenia is the same, but one of the common symptoms is hearing voices.

The voices are real. They are louder than your television. They yell at you. You hear them as clearly as someone in front of your face. They tell you to stop, or go, or kill, or stop, go, stop, go, don't kill. Don't. Run away, come back, eat, don't eat. Be afraid.

You put your hands over your ears and turn round and round to escape, but you can't.

Ruth heard voices. But she also saw things, things that were real, things that anyone could see but many ignore. She told me she had been in the world outside the hospital and now was on the inside and there is no real difference.

"You never know," she said. "You never know." She smiled when she said that. She had a twinkle in her eye, so I know what she said was honest. She said "You never know" as she looked at people wandering the grounds of the hospital deep on drugs that kept them stable and vertical. They were also in a way comatose, except they were awake. All of this is insane, of course. Which is the problem.

Ruth was wise. Ruth was smart. Ruth figured out how to tie the shoelaces in her life by accepting the idea that you cannot know what is going to happen.

You never know what is going to happen, you never know what good thing or bad will come to you. You just never know, so you should not be surprised at anything that ever happens.

Is that deep, or mindless? I don't know. But I do know that whenever anything happens which is a surprise I say, "You never know." And that has often saved me from the shock that comes with triumph and disaster.

For Ruth, it eliminated the stress, the blame and the fear in her life. It was the only sane approach possible.

You should have skipped this story. I don't like writing or thinking about bad things. On the other hand, maybe you should read it again because bad things happen and you need a way to get through them.

The Hoarder (Who Saved Vancouver)

To Save the Past Is to Save the Future

N ot many liked him. He was arrogant. He easily got into arguments. He was a hoarder. If there had been reality television back then, someone would have done an episode on him.

But the producers of the show would have argued with him, because … Well, because he was hard to get along with. If they asked to see his collections he would have said, "No. You might steal them. But if I do let you see them you have to store them for me. And after that you can't claim they are yours. Understand?!"

He was not an easy person to deal with.

The Major had been in World War I and came back as a major. Most other captains and majors and colonels who come back from wars take off their uniforms and give up the additions to their names. They know people wearing civilian clothes would laugh at them.

Not Major Matthews. No one laughed at Major Matthews. No one would dare, or they would see a scowling face that would make them drop to the ground for ten push-ups.

Yes, he was demanding and overriding, as a major would be.

That may give you a hint of his personality.

His background was similar to many who lived in Vancouver in the city's early years. He was born in Wales. On his way to Vancouver he lived in New Zealand. He arrived in Vancouver when the city was twelve years old, in 1898. A decade and a half later came the war and out of it came the Major.

But most of all Major Matthews was a collector.

He collected everything. Nails. Shoes. Letters. Pictures. The only theme he had was that the things he collected had to come from Vancouver.

If someone was throwing out stuff from their damp cellar, the Major was there.

"Can I have it?"

"It's useless. Junk."

"Can I have it?"

"If you want. It's on its way to the dump."

If he found something on the street—a horseshoe, a hat—he picked it up and it would join his collection.

He especially liked pictures. He collected half a million of them, all of early Vancouver. Can you imagine half a million pictures, most on paper? You could not get half a million pictures into your bedroom, even if it were a master bedroom, without spilling over into your ensuite and your garage.

You would not be popular at home.

The pictures were of horses, cows, trees, people riding horses, milking cows and cutting down trees. Almost all one of a kind. There were few negatives back then.

What's a negative?

That is the young people asking. Or not asking because *negative* is a foreign word and they skipped over it.

A negative, dear children of the iPhone age, is a piece of plastic film on which an image was recorded inside a camera. But it was backwards. The lights were dark and the darks were light. You can look at it, but it is hard to make sense of it.

When a picture was printed from the negative, the result was called a positive. Then the lights and darks were where they should be.

You are following this, right? Your grandparents understood it.

From a negative you got a picture that you could put into an album. What's an album?

That was a book in which you put your favourite pictures and later others would look through your album and say, "Wow. That was a wonderful time." You have probably seen these albums in your grandparents' home. You have looked through them and thought that was a nice way of showing pictures.

There were usually fifty or sixty pictures. You have ten thousand in your phone. (And no one sees them.)

I am telling you this to widen your understanding of life, and maybe help you win a game of Trivial Pursuit.

Before negatives, pictures were made mostly on glass plates which served as the negative, usually only leading to one print being made.

That was the world in which Major Matthews was collecting.

His friends would say things behind his back, the same as people always do. "The Major is a major nutcase. He's collecting these old buggy whips. Who would do that?"

In addition to the pictures, where did he find space for the army uniforms and garden tools and horseshoes and grocery store signs? That is what his wife wanted to know.

"We have filled all the closets and the basement and the attic and the bedrooms and the spaces under the beds. And if we had an ensuite (which we don't because they haven't been invented yet), that would be filled also."

So Major Matthews went to City Hall and this is where the story gets dramatic. The mayor let him put his collections into the big library at Main and Hastings, and in some storerooms at City Hall, and some other storage spaces around the city.

If you drive over the Burrard Bridge you can see one of those spaces. The things over your head that are supposed to look like castles were filled with the Major's collections. That is, until the pigeons got inside, and the rats, and the rain. The Major moved the collections out.

Before that, the mayor felt he was just helping out a nice old veteran and told the Major that he was the unofficial archivist of the city.

The mayor thought this was a compliment. The Major thought it was an insult. He wanted to be the *official* archivist. The city had no position called official archivist.

You think this is a small deal? The Major did not. He was hurt, but he needed the city's storage space.

After a while, a long while, the mayor told the Major that since the city was storing all this stuff, it legally belonged to the city. I suspect that was a way to get rid of all that junk and use the storage space for city council meeting minutes.

The Major leaned his face into the mayor's face and screamed, "What the [blank] are you, you [blank] [blank] talking about, you [blank]?!"

The mayor said something along the lines of, "It's our space."

The Major said something along the lines of: "My collection will be remembered longer than you will, you [blank]!"

The Major grabbed all his stuff and with the help of some friends brought it back to his house.

His wife said ... We don't know what she said, but we know she said it and we know the Major did not hear it.

What was in his collection? Basically every picture of early Vancouver. The pictures of men on a log selling real estate after the big fire. The picture of Maple Tree Square when Gassy Jack's saloon was the meeting place of the tiny town. And every picture of every stump of every unbelievably giant tree that was chopped down by hand, with the woodsmen standing next to the stump.

Those pictures are truly, unquestionably, and you can't believe how irreplaceable. And many of them would have been sent to the dump if it wasn't for the Major.

The Major also interviewed people. When I read what he did I said, "Right on! That's what I do." He did not talk to politicians. They come, pretend they have powers above the masses, pretend to have deep thoughts, pretend what they do is important, then go away and are forgotten. Instead, the Major talked to ordinary people, those who didn't pretend to be someone they weren't.

He talked to a woman who told him about coming home from a Boxing Day party in 1889. He talked to her forty-four years after it happened. She told him that their little merrymaking group was singing and strolling when a large branch from a tree suddenly broke and fell on them.

Four were killed. Two escaped. It happened at what is now Marine Drive and Argyle Street.

It is sad. It is terrible. But if it was not for the Major those lives would have no recorded history. Does that matter, even if no one knows them?

Yes.

The woman he spoke to was Miss E.J. Rowling. There is no record of anything else in her life. But on the other hand, there is this record.

Major Matthews talked to everyone he could. He wrote their stories on a manual typewriter using onion skin paper.

Okay, folks. Some history. Onion skin paper was used by your grandparents, like me, to make letters weigh less. The paper was—guess—onion skin thin. It was hard to write on but those who used it survived. They knew the receiver would be happy to read a real message that was about more than what the sender had for lunch.

The Major wrote 3,300 pages single-spaced, on onion skin paper, of interviews with real people who lived in the early years of Vancouver. I envy him. When the pages were put into books they were seven volumes thick. I don't envy that.

Later the city officials had a look at his collection and said, "Wait a minute. Has anyone looked at this stuff? Does anyone know what it is? And more importantly, do we own any of it?"

The city staff said simply: "No. It all belongs to Major Matthews."

Then the city officials said, wisely, belatedly, "Maybe we should grab it before some foreign buyers get it and try to sell it back to us."

Someone wise at City Hall called Major Matthews and asked him to donate his collection to the city.

There was one thing he would get in return, and only one thing. He would be the first *official* city archivist.

The Major said what a good military officer would say: "Yes, sir."

You can see all of his pictures, and you really should, at the city's archives, which is in Vanier Park, which is behind the planetarium in a building named the Major Matthews Building. Finally, a place to put all his stuff.

The Major's wife would be so happy.

It is also the *official* archives. The Major would be so very happy.

The Marine Building

You Never Know, So Do Not Be Surprised

M ost of the history stories I've written are in another book. That is where I met a man who never dies—which is not a bad thing. It's given him time to pay off his Visa.

He told me stories of good people and bad who he met in the old days of this city.

There was Ben Rogers of the sugar company. He was a bum.

And Pauline Johnson who dreamed up the name Lost Lagoon. She was a sweetheart.

But one thing he did not tell me was the story of the Marine Building.

That's the giant bricks-and-mortar ice cream cake on Burrard Street.

The building is a lesson in the most basic rule of life: You never know.

I first heard that from a woman at Riverview Hospital, where I spent much time reporting.

For those of you who are young, that was the mental hospital. It went by many other names, all unkind. People in any kind of hospital should not be mocked.

You read about this a few stories ago, unless you are skipping around, which is what I do when I read a book like this.

What I learned from Ruth: Don't be surprised. Don't be angry. Don't be upset. Just do the best you can. Don't think you have superpowers for winning at poker.

Don't think because a romantic interest smiles at you that you will have a beautiful life. Don't think because things are bad you will have a terrible life.

Don't think you have your future planned, because you never know.

Don't think that if you build the tallest, most beautiful building in the city with the intent of getting rich off it, that your plan will actually work.

And that is what happened with the Marine Building.

In 1880 the area around Burrard Inlet was home to only a few hundred white folks. They were the early undocumented immigrants. Thirty years later it was home to one hundred thousand. You never know what will happen.

Beer makers and real estate agents were the big winners. That, you could have guessed. Twenty years later, in 1930, downtown was getting crowded. The rich were buying big houses in Blue Blood Alley, which was West Georgia. They were getting rich selling trees and fish.

The cutters of the trees and the catchers of the fish were just getting by. They lived in the Eastside, a long commute from work.

If this sounds like today, it is because it sounds like today.

The rich said, "Let us build a building where buyers and sellers can buy and sell with contracts and deeds and signatures, and we will get richer and never get our hands dirty."

And they built a building next to the sea, and because it was there they called it the Marine Building. It was twenty-two stories high. It almost touched the clouds.

They made it beautiful, and it really was and is. You can go into the lobby and say, "Wow! That is beautiful."

They spent more money than they had budgeted, but they said, "That does not matter. We will make more."

They opened the building and the stock market crashed.

And the world went into depression. No one rented any of the offices in which to buy and sell things to make more money. And the towering luxury building that looks like an ice cream cake was empty.

Even the main fellow who ran the building could not afford the rent.

No income. No budget. Nothing. There was nothing the builders of the building could do except sell the building, for thirty cents on the dollar.

But it is still beautiful.

They did not know or suspect or plan for what would happen. But it happens. Ruth from Riverview could have told them.

Harry Figured It Out

If You Figure Out How to Do Something, Don't Hide It

H arry Houdini hung upside down out an office window in
Vancouver in 1923. I had a still picture of this. I was happy. I
thought I could do a story on it, because Houdini was a fascinating character.

But I could not do a story because I had only the one picture. I had
found pictures of Houdini in chains and handcuffs, but they were not
taken in Vancouver and they were not as exciting as someone hanging
upside down in a straightjacket. Having only one picture was a problem.

I mentioned this to one of the editors, Dylan Baker. He had good
training to be an editor: He was a rock and roll singer in his own band
and a bartender.

Bartenders know everything because everyone tells them their
secrets and problems. That's a lot to know. Rock singers know everything because they make a living off everyone's secrets and problems.

And they know how to hold on to a crowd by making an art out of
those human conditions.

A good editor knows everything because editors have heard every
secret and problem from everyone in every story they have edited. And
they know how to hold on to a crowd by—you guessed it—making an
art out of those human conditions.

But it takes a lot of listening before you get even a little learning.

Anyway, Dylan—bartender, singer, editor—saved Houdini, at least
for me.

He came up with two minutes of film, from 1923, of Houdini hanging out a window in Vancouver in a straightjacket and getting out of it.

What else could I hope for?

Now, about those jackets. They were evil things designed to keep the mentally ill restrained. What they really did was make them go crazy.

Someone made you push your arms in the sleeves, and then they would cross your arms over your chest and pull the straps tight around the sides of your body. That held you up straight. Your head was locked in place by a collar of heavy canvas and you could not move.

"There you go, Governor, see you in a week."

Harry Houdini made a living from the straightjacket.

Why? Easy answer. After his family left Eastern Europe they lived in dire poverty in America. They were Jewish. Work was hard to find.

You are not like Harry Houdini if you were born in Canada and you are a white Christian.

If you lived one hundred years ago, and your parents were Jews from Eastern Europe like Harry's (or Catholics from Ireland, Hindus or Sikhs from India, or Muslims from anywhere), then forget finding decent work.

You would be in a laundry, or restaurant, or factory. And you would be in the back where no one would see you.

But Harry wanted to do something amazing. He wanted to beat the odds. He wanted to escape the chains of prejudice. His way was to be a magician. Why? Because he had seen some magicians and wanted to do what they did. How do most of us choose our careers? And most of all, that would keep him out of the factories.

Trouble was, Harry was not very good at making magic.

But he was good at picking locks, which is a very good talent if you want to break into houses. Harry did not want that. He wanted to make an honest living. So he figured out how to get out of handcuffs.

That was a living made by doing what you were not supposed to be able to do.

He got better and better at it. But all shows need publicity. And that is what led Harry to the straightjacket. He figured out how to escape from it and, more than that, he figured out how to get famous doing it.

And this is where Dylan's film came alive. It was a complete recording of Harry getting hoisted up the side of what is now the Sun Tower.

It had a different name back then, but it was the tallest building in the British Empire, so it was a good stage to perform on.

Harry gave this show away for free. And of course he did it outdoors, where he would get the biggest audience.

He got the local police to put him into the jacket. That would insure no cheating (and there was no cheating). Then his feet were tied and he was hoisted upside down by a crane and he dangled above the crowd.

That is amazing just on its own and also it has got to be the craziest idea ever in the history of the world. Of course, if he could not do it, he would have been the biggest letdown in the history of advertising.

But what publicity.

As the police were tying the jacket tight Harry took many deep breaths. He was an extremely powerful man. He could expand his chest a great deal and hold his breath for at least three minutes. You can see him taking the deep breaths in the film.

When he let the air out, his chest shrank, and it gave him a tiny bit of wriggle room. Then as he was being hauled up above the crowd he forced his shoulders out of their sockets.

Ouch. Worse than ouch. Have you ever had a dislocated shoulder? Pain. But that way he could move his arms enough to get them out of the sleeves.

This was not a cheap trick.

After his arms were loose he swung his upper body up—basically doing sit-ups upside down with dislocated shoulders—until he could grab the jacket's outside straps with his teeth, and then he yanked.

The first time he did it, he took an hour and a half. It would be hard to keep an audience interested that long, even when you are doing the impossible. But by the time he got to Vancouver he could do it in three minutes.

That was how he made a living. A lot more exciting than working in a factory.

He got out of his straightjacket and raised his arms upside down and the crowd cheered. And at night he went on stage at the sold-out Pantages Theatre in front of paying crowds and wowed the audience by slipping out of chains and handcuffs. The straightjacket promo worked like magic.

Not a bad gig.

And Dylan and I had a story suitable for evening television.

But not really.

Dylan knew a cheering crowd was good. But he said good rock groups always had an extra song. When the show was over it still needed to go on, just for a bit.

"What's *new* about this?" he asked, about the ninety-five-year-old event.

"The police would now never get involved with anything like this," he went on without pausing.

I was happy with leaving Harry being cheered.

"And WorkSafeBC would never allow a crowd like this to stand under a man dangling on a rope," he said.

"And," finally I said something, "the city would never allow this without a waiver of liability from Harry."

I was happy. Dylan thought of almost everything. I had thought of something.

Dylan and I were both talking now, and from his bartender experience his field of expertise was endless: "He would need a safety net," said Dylan. "And the fire department would have to be on the scene and ambulances would need to be nearby and there would need to be special constables for crowd control and extra police would be needed for security and news organizations would need to be kept back for their safety, but not too far back because Mr. Houdini would demand they be up close."

And that was just the beginning. Food trucks would need special permits to be there, and porta-potties would have to be rented, and the crane operator would need a backup crane operator, and—wait a minute, is it legal for a crane to operate on weekends and can he legally dangle a human being? And what about the straightjacket? Where do we get one of those? The only place they might exist is in some museum of the macabre, and would they allow it to be used in something that might ruin it?

That is what editors do. They do not go out into the rain and the storms, they sit in little rooms with pictures and brainstorm. Sometimes it can tire them out as much as holding an umbrella against the wind. Again, I have said this many times: Everyone needs an editor.

And we concluded that this impossible event, which you have just seen become possible in an old film, would now be impossible to recreate because of rules and regulations.

And that was the story you saw, not just the escape, but the irony of not being able to escape now.

Stories, like shoelaces and straightjackets and chains, can get tangled right before your eyes, and sometimes need help to straighten them out.

Sister Frances

You Don't Need School to Learn Being Good

Frances Street is just six blocks long. It is south of Hastings between Vernon and Victoria.

Unless you live there, who cares? That's what I thought. The street is almost all apartment buildings with one shop that sells turbochargers and fuel injectors.

Those are expensive additions to cars for those who recently got their licence and have their first legal taste of speed, and whose main goal is to shorten the driving time between red lights.

Who was Frances? Don't know? People who live on the street don't know. People who used to live on the street don't know.

You are about to be impressed. The street is named after an exaggerator, a fibber—if we used our current descriptions, a resumé inflator.

On the other hand, she was a war hero and a saint.

Sister Frances Redmond was born in Northern Ireland in the middle of the nineteenth century. She volunteered as a nurse in the Boer War in South Africa. That is so easy to write and to read. Can you imagine actually doing it?

She was brave. She was wounded. She is one of very few women to win the Victoria Cross. That alone would be a life's work.

Then she married. Women who married in the 1800s entered a life of having babies and cooking and cleaning and having more babies.

Frances had two. And she and her husband moved to Canada. They stopped in Winnipeg for a few years where she studied nursing and started feeling a devotion to the Anglican Church. Maybe because of that, or maybe because they just argued a lot, she and her husband separated.

That made her a single mother. Not many women had that designation back then. It would have been close to impossible to survive.

Shortly after the great fire in Vancouver she got a letter from a church friend who asked her to help with the medical and religious needs of that tiny, frontier sawmill town.

There were only 8,500 souls here—mostly men—and many who drank a lot, and even more who got injured in the mills and the woods. There were women too, but there was no care for them, or their children or any other problems they might face. It was a tough place.

There were some wealthy people who made fortunes off the sawmills and the railroad that had just arrived in the city, but they lived on the west side of town.

Frances moved to the east side.

She wanted to be a deaconess, which is a non-ordained member of the church who devotes her life to others, kind of like a nun without being a nun. She said she had been educated to be such a person, but there actually were no places teaching it in Canada until four years later.

Still she said she was a fully schooled deaconess of the church and she added "Sister" to her name. She made up her own vow to help the sick and the poor. She dressed for the rest of her life as an Anglican nun.

She ministered to everyone, but especially women. She was the busiest midwife in town. She claimed she had learned midwifery at Laval University in Montreal, but no woman was admitted to Laval until ten years later.

Okay, so you have to cut her some slack because she got people together to start the building of the city's first hospital, a block from Oppenheimer Park, which even then was a poor area. The hospital had seven beds and she cared for those in each of them.

She worked with little sleep during a smallpox epidemic. She cared for typhoid victims.

She sat on her luggage in a stagecoach all the way to Lytton to care for the sick.

She devoted her life to serving others. She was true to her own vow. She was called the Florence Nightingale of Canada.

Her daughter died as a child. Her son was killed in World War I. She raised three orphans.

She was honoured with Vancouver's Good Citizen Medal in 1928 in a giant ceremony in English Bay attended by thousands.

And she died shortly after that at seventy-eight, suffering in great pain from cancer.

When you walk on Frances Street maybe you can feel something even more powerful than a turbocharger, like a sister who was a saint. No one needed to check her resumé.

Reilly

*An Old Story Is Like an Old Friend—You
Keep Going Back for New Advice*

And then I met Reilly. Every talk I have given, every book I have
written has been about Reilly.

Just in the unlikely—almost impossible—possibility that you
haven't heard this before: I am about to save your life.

If you do know the story you know that it is true. Every time it is
late and I have not yet found something for the news I think of Reilly
and I find something. Every time I am not feeling well I think of him
and I am fine.

I was at Trout Lake, which is a park in East Van. The poor people's
park, or at least it used to be.

The houses of the poor people are now worth millions. Lucky them.
Wish I had one. Or at least I wish I lived near Trout Lake.

Let us start with some good advice. If you live in Greater Vancouver,
go to Trout Lake. It is at Sixteenth Avenue and Victoria Drive. You can
park there. Parking is free. There will be no tourists or people playing
golf. It is still a park for the people, except the people are the luckiest
ones on earth, or at least the luckiest ones in East Vancouver.

There is a lake in the middle of the park and I was looking across
it for something. Anything. And there was something: a kid, fishing.

There is nothing better. In an age of computer games, it was wonderful to see a kid with a real game, a real puzzle, a real contest. Of course,
this particular game had a problem—as all things have—since Trout
Lake is the only lake or pond in Metro Vancouver that is not, repeat
not, stocked with trout.

So here was this kid trying to do the impossible, which is a good place to begin.

There are no fish because one end of the pond is reserved for dogs. The folks here do not just have an unleashed dog area, they have an unleashed dog dive-into-cool-water-and-swim-after-the-stick area.

Hence, no fish.

And there was Reilly, who I did not know was Reilly.

He had a fishing pole, which was a stick with leaves still growing out of it, and a string, which was hemp with threads sticking out of it.

Pretty good. Hollywood could not make anything better.

I shouted to him asking if his mother was nearby.

He answered, haltingly, "My foster mother ..."

And I knew we would have a problem. His speech was strained, which means he had problems, and when he said his foster mother, I knew those problems were deep.

I have told this story over and over, but give me a second. If you know this part of it, good. It should remind you how lucky you are. If not, read on.

Foster parents have saved the world. Most are good. All have replaced the warehousing of kids in orphanages. When I was young there were still orphanages and we were always told, "Be careful of the kids in there. They are extra tough because they have no parents. If you get into a fight with them they might kill you because no one is going to get mad at them for doing that."

That is a reputation hard to live up to, unless you want to be a boxer, a bouncer or the head of a corporation.

Foster parents did away with orphanages. They raised the kids more or less as their own. Sometimes bad, usually good, but never like in an orphanage.

So this kid had no parents that he could go home to and he had problems talking and he was about nine years old. Not a good start to life.

I talked to his foster mother, who was sitting nearby reading a book, and she said sure we could talk to Reilly.

I now knew his name.

I squatted down on the narrow dock and asked if he had caught any fish.

There is more to the story, mostly about his runny nose, but we will skip that now. The important part was his answer:

"No, but I believe …" and there was a long pause after that with a sniffling nose and a search for words. Then he added, "I believe if you believe you can do something …" and there was another pause and another sniffle. "You can do anything," sniffle, pause, "if you believe you can."

That is a powerful answer.

I asked the same thing about getting even a nibble. And he replied with the same words.

That was the beginning, middle and end of the story. When it went on the air it was beautiful. A little autistic Jesus, or Buddha or Muhammad.

Someone called me and offered to give him a new fishing rod. I called his home and his foster mother spoke to Reilly, then told me that he said, "No thank you." He wanted to catch a fish with his own rod.

All of that is a nice story. Without getting tedious, I started to repeat what Reilly had said to me.

I believe I can find a story. I believe I can be good to my family members. I believe I can be good to others. I believe I can be healthy. I believe I can be happy.

I don't believe I can win the lottery. Let's get real. I only believe I can do things that I have some control over. And once I am happy and getting along with most others and doing what I like, I basically *have* won the lottery.

After I started believing I could find a new story for TV every day I started finding a new story every day. After I started believing I could be good to others I was as good as I could be. And after I started believing I would be healthy I was healthy.

No, I am not a Pollyanna, no the world is not all good, but I do find something more or less good to talk about most days—and so can you—and I do get along with most others, and even when I get hurt or sick I get better.

I don't change reality. I just change the way I see it.

That is why Reilly is in every talk.

I never saw him again. But I know he caught a fish, somewhere.

Little Litter

Looking Good Does Not Mean You Are (Ancient Saying)

She put her hand around her back and dropped the tissue paper.
No one could see it, she thought.

She was very pretty. She was well dressed.

No one would blame her. No one would say, "Hey, that's littering!" because she looked so good and she knew it.

Then she got out another tissue and blew her nose again.

And thought, "No one will see me," and she dropped her tissue.

She had carefully chosen her clothes for the day, matching dress and coat and shoes. She looked in the mirror. "I'm a killer star," she might have thought.

And then she walked away from the tissues on the ground and some who saw them lying there might have wondered if it was some ugly, poor slob who dropped them.

No, we should not blame the ugly, poor slob. Just blame a jerk in a pretty dress who possibly thought no one as nice-looking as her would ever be accused of littering. The ugly, poor slob looked very good in comparison.

Hope

No Matter How Stormy There's Always a Break

The nicest thing. I am sitting here writing in a room where much has been written. There are piles of papers around me. Literally piles. I have been writing since before computers, which did away with piles of paper.

My wife would like me to get rid of the piles, but I say, "Suppose there is something in there that is worth reading?"

And she says, "Are you kidding? If it's worth it you already sent it to the publisher of Harbour, who has read many things that are not worth reading.

"So please get rid of those piles."

"But just suppose."

"No, get rid of them."

And then I see the recycling truck from Smithrite pull up outside. I stand up to watch someone doing real work. I am protected by curtains. He cannot see me.

The fellow gets out, as he will do hundreds of times today, takes a few steps back and grabs my blue box with plastics and yellow bag with papers, lots of papers.

I think, "He is larger than most who do this job and he has to haul that extra weight around each time he stops. That is a lot of work." I think, after looking at him, that I will lose weight. That is an important thing to learn from a recycling guy seen from behind a sheer curtain.

With one in each hand he dumps the box of cans into one slot and empties the bag of papers into another, then drops the box on top of the yellow bag, which is nice, and he takes five steps back to the open door of the truck.

But after he dumped the yellow bag in the slot, I saw one piece of paper float out behind him. I think, in a nanosecond of thinking, that I will go out later and pick up that paper.

I am not annoyed or disappointed or anything. Heck, this guy does this same stop-and-go and in-and-out and picking up and dumping out and putting back and going and stopping all day. I have not worked that hard since I pumped gas in a taxi garage when I was sixteen.

The paper fell behind him. He did not see it. But then, through the curtains, I see him stop. He did see it, with his wonderful peripheral vision.

That is the amazing ability we all have of seeing things on the sides of our heads. Kung fu fighters develop this so well it looks like they know when someone is attacking them from the side when it is impossible to know that.

And some old men learn it when they are on a bus and a twenty-something sits next to them.

The recycling guy stops just before he steps up into the truck. He pauses a second. He turns and walks back to the piece of paper and picks it up and throws it into the slot for papers.

If you have ever had a negative thought about the future of humanity, forget it. This is what the Buddhists preach, though the Buddhists do not preach, and what the Catholics preach and the Jews and Muslims and Jehovah's Witnesses and Masons—yes, the Masons do preach about being good and kind—this was everything in one.

Let me detour again. Sorry, but this is important and probably the last time I will get to tell this story.

It was in an earlier book, but heck, you may have missed it.

After my mother left my father, I was raised for a while by an uncle who was a bus driver and a Mason. I knew what bus drivers did. I did not know what Masons did.

Later he became a driving instructor for bus drivers so he must have been pretty good. But the only thing I knew about his Masonic life was he would take his sacred books and go into a closet to read them.

Can you image a top-floor apartment in New York in the summer under a flat tar roof? I don't have to imagine. It was hot in the apartment even with windows open and fans going. In a closet it was unimaginable.

But he was supposed to study in secret. I learned that later. All I remember was him carrying a book wrapped in cloth going in, and then later, sweating, him coming out while wrapping up the book in the same cloth.

He was a thirty-third degree Mason, the highest you could be without becoming a Shriner, which he detested. I know that because he told me so even though I had no idea what a Shriner was.

Much later in my reporting life I learned that Shriners are among the world's best people. They dress in clown costumes and ride tiny motorcycles and raise money for sick children.

They run one of the world's largest hospitals and charge nothing for those who use it. They are like saints—but I think it was the clown costumes that my Uncle Ed did not like.

He wore brown clothes all his life. During the 1960s, when long hair was growing everywhere, he told me that he combed his hair with a part just there in the middle, the same as he had done all his life, and he would keep it there for the rest of his life. And his hair would never touch his ears. That was commitment.

He raised me during one of the periods when I was difficult to raise. When my mother and I moved out of his and his wife's and son's apartment we lived only walking distance away and he continued to be the father in my life when I had no father.

Later, after I moved to Vancouver, he died. It happens. I needed to go to his funeral. It was late at night when I got the call.

The next day I got a flight, but it would not get to New York until late in the afternoon. That was just before the casket would be closed.

When we landed I, along with all the passengers, learned that the New York taxicab industry had gone on strike. Those were the famous yellow cabs, of which there were millions, almost, and they were the lifeblood of the city.

There was no other way to get from the airport to the funeral home in Queens, which is not Manhattan where all the buses went. The buses were the only things still moving.

That would mean I would take a bus to Manhattan, then take the subway back to Queens by which time the casket would be closed and the funeral home would be dark.

I got on a bus and sat, dejected. I was not hiding my dejection.

The driver asked what was wrong. This was amazing. In New York a bus driver speaking to a passenger does not happen. There are too many passengers and too many drivers.

I told him my uncle was dead and I was not going to get to the funeral home in time. I told him where the funeral home was so he would see it was impossible.

"Sorry," he said. He was Hispanic, Puerto Rican, because basically every Hispanic person in New York then was Puerto Rican.

And all Puerto Ricans were hated by all white people and black people, which is the only way to think and run your life when you are growing up in a racially divided city, which I did. Think of the movie *West Side Story* to understand everything there is to know about racism.

Then I said, "He was a bus driver."

The Puerto Rican bus driver shook his head in sympathy, then closed the door and started off.

If you have ever landed at JFK Airport in New York you know—or you don't know—that in your rented car or on a bus you drive north on Van Wyck Expressway.

You probably don't know the name, but you have driven on it. It cuts into other roads, but basically it takes you straight into Manhattan where your high-rent apartment or overpriced hotel is waiting.

All the New Yorkers on the bus know this route. The driver pulled out of the airport onto Van Wyck and headed north. The bus was full. Many were standing, holding onto straps, thinking thoughts of getting home.

Then at the Jamaica Avenue exit, a few miles from the airport, the driver got into the exit lane. No bus had ever gotten off there.

I knew the street well. I had grown up nearby. Other passengers knew something was wrong. I saw their heads looking around, silently asking, "What the heck is going on?"

The bus pulled up to Jamaica Avenue and turned left. Now there was murmuring from some passengers. Either they were on the wrong bus, which was impossible because there was no other bus, or they were being kidnapped, which is not a good thing to happen on the way home.

The bus drove along Jamaica Avenue for half a dozen blocks before some passengers, and then more passengers, said to each other, but not to the driver because they would be afraid of confronting a Puerto Rican behind the wheel, "Where are we going?"

The driver said nothing and kept going. Ten blocks later he pulled over.

"The fellow going to the funeral, get off here. You can get another bus here."

I got my suitcase, I got up and I got off.

"Thank you," was all I said, which I hope he heard.

The bus pulled away and made a right turn at the next corner. It was headed back to the assigned route.

I knew my way. It was a long walk or a short bus ride. I ran, and I got to the funeral home just before they closed the box. I could hug my aunt who had lost a husband of sixty-five years.

But of course, you never know what is going to happen. A problem.

There was a discussion, no, an argument among my uncle's fellow Masons. The Masonic apron he was being buried with was the wrong apron.

It is their ritual that all Masons are buried with the apron that Masons traditionally wore to protect their clothes from the rough work of hammering on stones and that also had pockets to carry tools. It is a nice tradition.

But like all groups it has its rules. The final apron had to be a new one and the one on my uncle who was lying in his coffin was not new. Good heavens.

Rules.

Someone said he would drive to my aunt's apartment and get the new, unused one that her husband would wear forever.

This of course took enough time for me to have walked from the airport, almost.

Everything was taken care of, according to the rules, and I spent the rest of the night alone with my aunt in their apartment. And I looked through the curtains and venetian blinds and screens on her windows and was thankful to a bus driver from Puerto Rico.

Back to the recycling guy. The one who picked up the paper in front of my house.

He did what was good even though it slowed him down from a heavy, endless schedule.

The lesson: We the people, led by a recycling guy from Smithrite, and a bus driver from Puerto Rico, will survive and be okay.

The Garden

You Don't Have to Be Noticed for Doing Something Good

There is a planter outside the post office downtown on Georgia Street. I'm talking about the old post office which is a giant building. It was constructed in a time when people wrote letters.

The new post office is a block away. It takes up a corner of a building. Foreign exchange students now use it to pick up money sent from home after promising their parents that they are studying hard and not wasting their money on parties.

I have been meeting people, mostly camera operators, outside the old post office for ten years. And throughout that time, I have watched the planter on the corner of Georgia and Hamilton.

For a few years it was filled with garbage. It was easier to put a coffee cup in something high than it was to take two steps, reach down and put it in a steel garbage can.

My guess was that although it looked like it belonged to the post office, it was really more on the sidewalk than on postal property, so the maintenance people at the post office figured it was not their responsibility.

And I know the city crews that came by to empty the city's garbage can on the corner did not clean the planter because, well, obviously, it was not a city garbage can on the corner. That's pretty simple.

There were candy wrappers in it and Styrofoam cups, back when we had Styrofoam cups, and cigarette butts and banana peels. And there were weeds.

Somehow nature, being strong and patient, swallowed up the garbage. I watched the weeds cover up the litter, then the weeds died and rotted and there seemed to be an endless battle between the new garbage and the new weeds.

Then came this spring, the early months of it when it finally stopped raining and the planter looked clean, with just bare ground. Someone had obviously done something. That was nice.

I passed by it almost every day. And every day I saw little green things coming up. And the more green things that came up, the less people were putting litter into it.

It was either that or someone was removing the garbage. In either case, the little green things were getting bigger.

For a while I took a different route. Two weeks passed, then yesterday, Thursday, May 11, 2018, I stopped at the planter. Actually, the planter stopped me.

The light said "Walk," but I did not walk. The planter was filled with orange flowers. I know they were zinnias because I once grew them. They are as easy to grow as marigolds, but prettier.

It was beautiful. And there was no garbage. I wished I had taken pictures of the planter over the years and through the spring. That would have made such a nice story. But I had not done that.

It would have shown that bad things can become good, even simple things. But why would I take pictures of garbage in a planter? That would have been just pointing out something bad.

And even when it was cleaned, why would I take a picture? That would have been showing something as it should be, not something remarkable.

And now the planter is filled with flowers. I took a picture.

Whoever did this, thank you. You will not get credit for what you did, but I don't think you were doing it to get noticed.

You were doing it so that an ugly old garbage-filled planter could be filled with orange flowers. That was all. And that was everything.

The Mystery of a Universal Need

Pain Can Go When You Forget You Have to Go

H ad to go. Needed a bathroom. Needed a story, but mostly needed a bathroom.

Stop, please stop, at Costco.

We are downtown, ten minutes from Costco and I have a membership card and they have a bathroom. But we are closer to Granville Island.

Okay. Let's check the Fishermen's Warf, same road, and they have a bathroom and maybe we will find something.

Nothing. No one. Empty. The bathroom is at the end of the dock.

But look, there's stuff on the ground near a locker.

The fishermen have big lockers for their gear. Is someone cleaning it out? That would be a good story, I think.

No. Just getting something out for today. "But," says the fisherman, "I have a friend you should meet."

Irwin.

Fetal alcohol syndrome. I hear that and think, "Sad. It is not your fault and yet you suffer forever for what someone else did."

We meet Irwin. As is the case for all FAS sufferers, letters do not hide the pain. Shrunken face, few words, slow thoughts, hard life.

But Irwin works on the dock, which is good, better than not working and wondering why he can't get work. He does grunt jobs, cutting bait mostly, and moving stuff.

"Couldn't learn in school," he says. "Went to special classes. Still couldn't learn."

He lifts and carries. He moves things in and out of the locker, heavy things, helping his boss. He is working, and I am happy. It is a good story and gives hope. Someone who often can't do things is doing things.

His friend, his boss, the fisherman, asks if we want to come to his boat.

No. We are done, I think. We have the story. We have the pictures. We have the information.

But to be polite we go.

At his boat the fisherman teaches Irwin to put rubber bands on the claws of crabs. Hard work. Lots of pinches. Painful pinches.

And after he does this many times Irwin almost shouts, "I just did something I never did in school!"

"What did you do?" I ask, thinking he never learned in school how to keep crabs from pinching the fingers of those who would buy them.

And Irwin shouts, "I learned something."

The story went from good to great!

And we left.

Hurry. I have to get to a bathroom.

I had forgotten about it.

How does that happen?

Beets Radio Commercial

Miracle Food Is What You Eat

We have found an ingredient in beets.
It can help lower blood pressure, and therefore make your life better.

It is a little-known chemical, found by a researcher in a lab.

But how can you know you are getting enough of this amazing, life-changing chemical?

The answer: We have developed Super Beets!

We have isolated, extracted, dried and put it into capsules for you.

We start with organic beets and guarantee this extract to be pure!

If you send for our offer now, we will also send you indicator slips that will tell you how well Super Beets are surging through your body and improving your life.

Just moisten one indicator with your tongue and you can tell immediately how Super Beets are working for you. Does the strip turn red? Then it's working!

Not mentioned in the slick, fast-paced commercial is the reality that everyone who eats beets knows. After you eat them your mouth is red and any paper sticking in it will be red and the next day going to the bathroom everything will be red too.

And if it is your first time eating them you will think you are bleeding to death.

But no blood. Just red. Just beets.

It always happens.

Back to the commercial: The indicators will turn red, they say.

And you will say, "My Super Beets are *working*! I am so happy. I will order more. I must be feeling better."

And, as always, at the end of the commercial: "This product is not approved by the Food and Drug Administration and cannot treat, cure or prevent any disease."

But that part is said so fast, you cannot hear it.

Be well. Eat beets. Or any vegetables.

Old Crow

Kindness Grows Wherever It Is Fed

He had a twisted foot. It was curled into a ball. The other foot was twisted nearly as badly.

He could not hold on to a branch. A bird who cannot sit in a tree is on death row.

He could not walk. He hobbled.

Pain was there when the curled foot pressed on the wooden railing overlooking the beach. Crows don't complain. But if you watched the hobble, you felt the pain.

Tom, the lifeguard at Third Beach, started feeding him a year ago. Lunch for the crow was part of Tom's lunch. Mostly bread from his sandwich, but sometimes some of what was inside the sandwich.

He shared his lunch all summer long. That was a year ago.

"I was surprised when I came back to work this year and he was still here," Tom said. "I thought for sure he would die over the winter."

While we talked a woman walked to the railing and put food on the wooden board.

"I fed him during the bad weather," she said. "I came here every day and gave him this special mixture."

She showed us balls about the size of the tip of a pinky finger. They were made of meat and vitamins, she said. She got them from a speciality bird food store.

"I call him Gimpy."

She put some more meatballs on the railing and Gimpy hobbled close to her.

He picked up four in his beak, then tried for five. One fell out.

"He's always greedy," said the woman.

She laughed, because she had watched and learned about the crow. And maybe the crow was learning about the woman, too.

She could spend more time watching than Tom, who even during his lunch break was watching the water to keep others alive.

Gimpy managed to hold four balls in his beak, then flew away.

"He does that every time. He hides them in the grass," she said.

Gimpy landed in some high weeds and did what she said he would do. He pushed his meals under the grass then flew right back to the woman.

She put out more balls, but another crow with two powerful feet landed, cawing and gripping the edges of the railing with his claws. He picked up a meatball.

Gimpy screamed at the thief and they shot up in an air battle of twists and dives and shouts of outrage and threats. Translation not needed.

As much as Gimpy could not walk, his wings turned him into a fighter pilot.

Desperation can make you strong.

The thief crow fled, and Gimpy flew back to the railing, landing on the top of his curled toes. He was out of breath. A crow panting is a strange, sad sight.

More food, more hiding.

"I didn't know she did this," said Tom.

And while we talked the kind woman quietly left, without leaving her name and apparently not wanting questions or praise.

But all summer she kept coming back with her high-potency meals and all summer Tom added bread to the meat and Gimpy got through the days, eating and fighting and at night sleeping in the grass. He could not roost on a branch.

But he was only half sleeping. Coyotes and racoons eat anything they can catch, and they catch things on the ground.

Many people hate crows.

They don't sing pretty songs. They fly in large numbers. They are scary.

But Gimpy's friends knew better. And their help wasn't charity. They were just helping someone they knew.

It is a cliché, but it is true: What you get out of doing something for someone is always more than you put into it.

Then one day Gimpy was not there.

If the woman was still putting out food, it was gone before I got there. I never saw the food and I never saw the woman. If it had been left, another crow had taken it without a fight.

I knew all this because I saw nothing.

I knew no crow with twisted feet stopped the theft because I did not see it happen.

Crows don't often live in memories, except, I thought, for two people who said goodbye and wished him peace and freedom from pain. What I knew was they had each made the wait for that peace just a bit less painful.

Now the important part. And this may be the most important part of this book.

It proves everything that we think we know may not be so.

But you know it is true because you not only know it—and that is the basic reason most of us are sure of things—but you have checked and rechecked and then checked it again. And it is true, because you know it. So you tell others.

And then you find out it is not true.

Suppose this happens with things you believe about yourself, about why you drink or use drugs or why you can't get out of debt. And much later you find out your excuses for doing things were really in your imagination.

What do you do?

You teach yourself not to be so sure about what you are sure of. And not to be so adamant about what you are adamant about.

Now, about the crow.

Last November and December and January, when it was cold and there was a bit of snow I went looking for the crow. He was not there. Last February and March and April and May I went at least three times a week looking.

Third Beach is part of my regular route searching for something to tell you about. If the crow was still there, if someone was feeding him, I would have told you. But he was not there. Ever.

If you add up the times I looked it was at least eighty-four. Yes, I have a good life. But not when it came to the crow.

Not there, ever, so he must be dead. And so I wrote the story.

Then came June, and lifeguard season, and I went to see my friend Tom, who is now in his fifty-second year of saving lives.

"He's back, you know," he said to me before he said hello.

"The crow?"

"Well I'm not talking about the tide," he said.

"Stop!" I said "Stop the presses. Stop the book!"

We can't say something is dead if it is not dead. That is a basic rule of truth telling. I thought of removing the crow story from the book. But then I said, "Wait, this is important."

This is where I learned that everything that anybody or everybody knows to be true, might not be.

You know the people who phone in to talk shows on the radio and say, "What everyone is missing is the point that I am going to make"?

No.

You know the time when you said to your partner in life, "What you are doing is wrong. This is the right way."

No.

This is where you hear someone say that something is true because everyone knows it is true and it has never been anything except true so therefore don't you go saying it is not true.

So you start believing it is true. Except you find out later it is not true.

The good news is the crow is still alive. He was probably fed all winter by the woman who did not give her name. And now in the summer he will gain some weight sharing Tom the lifeguard's lunch.

The even better news, I have learned, and I bet you have too, is simply that we cannot be sure of everything we are absolutely sure of. I think that is very high wisdom. And that is important.

Thank you, crow.

One Fish

The Only Story I Really Cannot Get Out of My Mind

This is so sad. I would hate to read it. But I can't forget it.

It was a newspaper story about a fish. One of those Siamese fighting fish, which are sold in tiny bowls.

True, they don't need much oxygen. In the real world, they live in muddy puddles. So in our world they survive in softball-sized bowls, which fit neatly in an office or condo.

The story was about one fish with a name, Ulysses, a tough guy, living in a hotel.

After guests checked in they found a fish in a bowl in their room. The idea was they would have company. It was easier than a cat or a dog.

But this fish just stayed in the lower part of the bowl, not moving. Just breathing. Besides the fish there was nothing else in the bowl. One bowl, one fish.

The fellow who wrote the article was a naturalist. He studied fish and animals. He was at the hotel to attend a conference on animals.

The naturalist took a picture of the fish, which was easy because it stayed still, just above the bottom of the bowl, and he wrote a scientific paper about it.

The bottom fin of the fish almost touched the bottom of the bowl.

The fish had nothing to do. Nothing to see. Nothing to nibble. Nothing to explore. Nothing to look at. Again, nothing to do.

The naturalist watched the fish for two days. It never moved.

He was told that it was fed by the cleaner, but that was when he was away at his conference.

On his last day he dropped a pebble into the bowl. He had found the pebble outside the hotel.

The fish dove down and poked at it. And tried to push it and swam around it and went to the top of the bowl then dove down to it. The fish came alive.

The fish had something to do.

The naturalist knew when he checked out they would probably take away the pebble because foreign objects could cause problems.

So sad. So much we could learn from a fish and a pebble.

Fit Collar for Dogs

Someone Said Craziness Knows No Limits, and Someone Is Right

I t's even better than my fit band," she said. "Now I know where Ozzie is all the time."

It was a commercial.

"He's kind of an escape artist."

"She's an idiot," I thought in my humble, non-accusatory way. She's proud her dog runs away.

But she has a new toy that lets her find him. How about a leash? How about training him not to run? How about getting a turtle? But then you could not do this ad.

She was talking about an exercise tracking device like many got for Christmas and stopped wearing by February.

It's a thrill at first to see how many steps you've taken and how many calories you've burned and how much better everything will be now.

Then comes the thought, "*That's it.* I'm not letting this thing rule my life." So the makers of the exercise trackers came up with a better idea. Make one for your dog.

You don't have to admit to yourself you are giving him too much food or too little exercise. You can have someone else do that.

But just wait. Soon: "*That's it, once again.* I'm not letting my dog's numbers rule my life! Take that thing off!

"Ozzie, go chase the ball. We both like that."

George Royal

A Slow Start Does Not Mean You Are Behind

He would not run. Not him. Not now.

The gate opened, but he was like a cow.

He would not run. He would not bow to the rider on his back.

The other horses ran. He was happy at the gate.

And then this horse named George Royal said, "Okay, what the heck, I'll run at a speed that is breakneck."

And he passed all those who started ahead and beat them by a mile, or two.

He did this every race. What a nutcase.

Then this Canadian horse went to California and met a famous jockey who had grown up in Canada. "We will be friends," the jockey said. "Even if you are different."

And the horse won and won and won, but then the horse grew old, and lost and lost and lost. The jockey also grew old, of course.

The jockey had ridden other horses, but for his last race he said to the old horse, I will ride with you.

His friends said, "No. For your last race? You need to ride a winner."

But the jockey said, "I like this horse. He is old, like me."

And at the jockey's last race and the horse's last race the horse stood at the starting gate for just a second after the gate opened.

Then he tore up the track to the finish line and won, just like when he was young.

If you go to the Hastings Racecourse and see a statue of an ordinary-looking brown horse in the paddock where the other horses walk around before the races start, that is George Royal, the horse who would not run. The fastest horse of all.

Go, Johnny, Go

And the Rider Who Almost Did Not Ride

You never know. Once again those few words encompass more of what happens in life than any other phrase I know.

The jockey who rode George Royal in his final race was one of the best in the world. No, actually, he was the best.

He was Johnny Longden. If you do not go to the racetrack the name will mean nothing. But if we were talking boxing, he was Muhammad Ali; baseball, Babe Ruth; hockey—and I know you know this—he was Terry Sawchuk, Gordie Howe, Mario Lemieux, Wayne Gretzky, Bobby Orr, Jean Béliveau, Maurice Richard or Grant Fuhr. Now you know.

In the middle of the twentieth century he had won more races than any other jockey, ever. During forty years of riding, which takes incredible strength and determination, he rode in 32,413 races.

He won 6,032 of them. That is one out of five times. In horse racing that is impossible.

He won the Triple Crown in 1943. Only twelve other jockeys in all of North American horse racing have done that.

And he was a nice guy.

A little of his history. He was born in England in 1907. When he was two his father came to Canada for a better life and three years later had made enough money to send for his wife and son.

I'll just skip ahead a little. Johnny's parents settled for a while in Alberta where the young boy grew up working in the mines. Later they moved to Vancouver, and that's where Johnny's love of horses came about.

When he was twenty, in 1927, he moved to California to join the state's rapidly growing racing culture.

He won his first race in his first year. In the 1960s he met George Royal, who had been brought down to California from Vancouver.

"You're Canadian, I'm Canadian. I know you have a crazy way of starting races, but we will try together," he said, or something like that.

And together they won. And after that they won, and kept on winning, always with George slow out of the gate.

Time passed and George Royal slowed down and lost. And then lost again. It happens when you get old.

On Johnny's last race in 1966, when he was fifty-nine (imagine holding on to the sides of a horse with your knees going sixty kilometres an hour, being surrounded by other horses and riders, all of whom want to get past you, knowing if you fall you will be stomped on by feet with pieces of metal nailed to them, and realizing you are just a few months from being sixty), he rode George Royal.

And despite being told not to ride him because his friends wanted him to end on a high note, Johnny climbed onto the saddle and guided his horse to the starting gate.

He not only wanted to ride George Royal because as he said, "You are old and I am old." And he did say that. And he not only picked George Royal because of the nostalgia for riding him when he first went to California. But he rode him, he said, because, "You are from Canada and I am from Canada." And yes, he said that, too.

And the gate opened and George Royal did what he always did. He did nothing, at least not for a long second or two. And if you are that far behind in any race you cannot make up the time.

That is unless you are George Royal and Johnny Longden.

Johnny looked at the backs of the other horses. But after one mile he was number seven. At the far turn he was number five. And then in the stretch to the finish he moved up and up until he and one other horse were nose and nose.

They crossed the finish line one nose ahead of the other.

A famous painting of that finish is hung in the lobby at the track at Santa Anita. People still talk about the horse that came up from behind to win with the rider who would not give up on him.

George Royal.

Back to Johnny and his mother moving to Canada. His mother was in a panic. They were on a train in England going to the docks. The train was late. If they missed the connection the ship would leave and all heck would happen.

Could they get the money back for their tickets? No.

If they did not get the money how could they buy tickets for the next ship? And if they missed it how could she let her husband know? She could not.

The train did not make up the lost time and they missed the ship. It pulled out without them.

The ship was the *Titanic*.

Johnny died happy, famous, wealthy and having lived a wonderful life, at ninety. If they had made it to the ship on time he would probably have been gone at five.

The Goat That Got Jazz

A Butt in the Butt Can Be a Pain in the ...

It should have been easy. Just take a bit of video of the goat while the goat does what goats do.

Except what exactly do goats do? Besides eating, there really is only one thing they do. They butt.

They have solid, strong, curved and pointed horns and they use them to get their point across. If you are in front of a goat you will get the point.

And this makes getting some video of a goat not easy. But I lied to Jazz Sanghera, the cameraman.

"It will be easy," I said. "You just point and shoot."

Of course I did not really say that. You never say that to anyone who works with a camera. It would be like telling a writer, "Just put down some words. That's all you do anyway, right?"

And then run. So I told Jazz, "It'll be easy. Just take your usual beautiful pictures."

And Jazz stood in front of the goat in the barn and raised his camera and the goat attacked.

Whoa. Sidestep. No. Don't be silly, you can't sidestep away from a goat.

Bang. Horns into butt because Jazz swung around to protect the part that the goat had been aiming for.

"Ouch!"

We were at the track inside one of the barns to see how a goat can calm a nervous racehorse. That is something goats do, which is hard to understand.

Goats are small. Horses are big. Goats have horns that could poke a horse in the nose and horses have hoofs clad with metal, under masses of muscle.

But it works.

Jazz tried again, and the goat tried again. This time Jazz did sidestep in time, but then the goat rebounded and came back for a second run.

"Ouch!" Again.

"Sorry," I said.

Jazz is as fearless as most news photographers. They get close to fires, floods and mindless people reading mindless press releases—which takes the most courage to contain themselves—all in a routine shift.

The problem is, goats are also fearless. Plus they are strong and fast and relentless and unforgiving. On the other hand, they are calming and friendly and devoted.

In short, they have the traits we hold dear.

When the goat got tired of Jazz he walked across the barn and into one of the stalls where a horse lowered its head and nuzzled his horns. The goat slowly moved his head to rub the horse's nose and the horse slowly stroked the horns with that same nose. They both avoided the pointed ends. They were lovers, in a horse-goat kind of way.

But what was the story? It was like everything in life. It was this and that.

It was when you went to the supermarket and saw someone you have not seen in years. They had open heart surgery, someone they knew but you did not know died, and they had a new grandchild. It is all those stories in one, plus picking up some carrots. You know that. You have spent a lifetime hearing and telling those stories.

And sometimes in retelling that trip to the supermarket the story gets so mixed up, the person you are telling it to can't tell if your friend had died or if your friend's friend had heart surgery or if someone's grandkids do not like carrots.

Our stories are everything mixed together and sometimes the main part never survives the first retelling.

The story on the air that night showed video of Jazz dodging a goat, which I took with my cellphone. It also had video of the goat nuzzling the horse, which Jazz shot.

Either story was good. Together they were wonderful.

Then the next day someone said, "I saw this goat and horse on TV last night. That was neat. I don't know what they were doing but I once heard that horses and goats like each other."

And that was good enough.

Hero Worship

Your Story Is Seldom as Good as Their Story

I was not a war hero.

I was newly married, meaning I had been married for two weeks, when the notice came. "Greetings," it said. If you are American and lived through the 1960s you knew those words. They proceeded: "You will report for a medical examination prior to your induction into the army."

It was not a good letter. Several of my friends had gone to Vietnam after they got those letters and, shortly after that, stopped living. Several others had stopped being friends because they came back different people.

One could not have any living thing close to him, not even a parakeet. He had killed people. Maybe people who were not soldiers. My wife-to-be and I had gone to see him and it was a sad and scary visit. We never went back.

I don't know what happened to him.

But my letter came and I did what my brother-in-law did and my cousin did. I left the letter on top of the radiator where I found it and went to see an air force recruiter.

The air force needed people too. So did the navy. And the chance of being one of the American soldiers who were itemized every night on the news was much less in the air force or navy.

I served. I was at a base, which I have talked about in earlier books, whose primary mission was to blow up Cuba. There was another war going on outside Vietnam. It was the Cold War, which was close to being very hot.

This was just a few years after the Cuban Missile Crisis, and if you do not know about that, please look it up. It was the closest the world ever came to blowing itself up.

Russia put missiles into Cuba and John F. Kennedy stood up to it. Read about it. You will get goose pimples. Kennedy won.

But afterwards, there was always the possibility that it would happen again. So the base I was at, along with every air force and navy base on the Gulf Coast of the US, was filled with supersonic airplanes that would attack whatever needed to be attacked in Cuba.

Red Alerts, meaning "Be ready for the worst to happen," were frequent.

But I did not have to face the Viet Cong shooting at me, which was nice.

Jump ahead twenty years. I am happy in Vancouver. I do television stories about things that happen. One of those things is the visit of the US Navy's *Coral Sea.*

It was an attack aircraft carrier. That meant it was small, as aircraft carriers go. Actually it was giant, but not like the truly giant ones. It was built to get places quickly and do its stuff.

This was before the attack on New York on September 11, 2001. Before that, the military liked to show off its muscles.

Before the attack on the World Trade Center, the world was basically open.

Before that I could wander around the police station and find stories. Before that I could talk to gardeners working for the city and learn about tulips. Before that I could go into recreation centres and ask what's new and be told about a barefoot Ping-Pong player.

After 9/11 everything closed up. I could no longer talk to gardeners about tulips without prior permission from the Park Board. I could no longer go into recreation centres without permission. And I could no longer walk past the front desk of the police station.

And no one could get close to anything military.

For better or worse, that is the world today.

But before 9/11 a visiting US Navy attack aircraft carrier was open to visitors, especially the media, who they hoped would do a positive story about them.

It was neat, interesting and what I liked most was watching the Marines, who always travelled with the ship, doing their exercises.

Marines are brave, tough and a lot of them die. They are the first in. They do things others don't do.

Those in the air force, the navy and the army have great respect for the Marines.

We watched them running around the decks of the ship with full packs and rifles. They did not get soft during a sea cruise.

Jump ahead twenty more years. It is good to grow old. You have many years in which to jump around.

I am in New Brighton Park looking at five people sitting around a picnic table. They are having lunch. They all have dogs that they walk in the park and they met there and after a while they decided to have lunch together one day a week.

The story was fine. In it there was salami and boiled eggs and tea and coffee and dogs and people.

"You should ask him what he did," someone said.

I did not get the name of "him." But I asked him.

"Nothing," he said.

"Yes, he did something," one of the others said. "He won the Silver Star."

If you are American and were in the military, you know the Silver Star is one step below the Medal of Honor. It is given only for the most heroic, brave and unbelievable things. You have to come *this* close, even closer, to dying, while saving someone or doing something that had to be done but was impossible to do.

The fellow, whose name I did not get, had a Silver Star.

He said he had been in the Marines.

How did you end up in Vancouver?

"I came in here on the *Coral Sea*," he said, "and I never saw such a beautiful place. I said when I retire I want to live here."

I could not remember the name *Coral Sea*. It did not twig in my mind. Things happen so fast when I am doing a story, or when any of us do anything. I was thinking only of the Sliver Star. I did not connect the name of the ship I was once on with him. I thought he was talking about a cruise ship that he might have come on sometime later in life.

I am fairly dumb.

I wrote the story and it was on television that night. It was about a group of friends who have dogs and have lunch, and one of them with white hair and a beat-up old comfortable jacket had won the Silver Star. That's pretty good.

And then driving home I remembered.

It came in a flash. "Darn," I thought. Darn. I wished I had remembered, and then I could have told him I saw him twenty years earlier running around the ship.

And then I thought, what difference would that have made? The story was about him, not me seeing him. His Silver Star was the important thing. It was about someone who got a letter saying, "Greetings," and instead of being drafted into the army went out and joined the Marines.

It was not about someone who visited a ship on which this Marine was running around the decks carrying a heavy knapsack and a rifle after doing something unbelievably brave.

I'm glad I did not remember.

War Story

Unexpected Kindness Is Better Than Killing

M y friend, Murray Titus, cameraman, big strong guy, was taking pictures of the cenotaph in Victory Square being cleaned.

City workers were power washing the ground, and without being overt, were moving drug dealers away.

"I'll tell you a story," he said. "I have a friend back home in Saint John."

That is New Brunswick where Murray was born, grew up, and went hunting and fishing with his grandfather—a more or less normal Maritime youth. Then he got into television, was sent to Kosovo, and learned how terrifying war is. It is hard to hold a camera on your shoulder when you have a helmet on your head. It is harder to take pictures when things in front of you are dying.

Murray is also this kind of guy: twice while I was working with him he stopped his search for the news of the day to help someone whose car had broken down. He went under the hood and helped get them going.

Unbeknownst to him I took pictures of him doing this, which became much better stories than anything we could find. You get the picture. He is a nice, and unusual, guy.

Now back to Saint John where Murray also made friends.

"Mike was number one," he said. "He would do anything for me and I would do the same."

That was Mike Burchill, his friend then and his friend decades later.

"It was right before Remembrance Day, like today, that Mike told me his father had been in the merchant navy in World War II. His ship was torpedoed by a U-boat."

I know that U-boats—that is, undersea war ships—sank more than three thousand freighters. That was their main prey. They were easy to attack, they had basically no defences except for a machine gun on the deck, and they were carrying war supplies to the Allies.

Three thousand ships sank. What is that? Only a number, but with them went forty thousand merchant—meaning civilian—sailors. That is a big, painful number.

The U-boats hunted in what were called wolfpacks. A few, or more, submarines would surround a fleet of slow-moving cargo ships, and all at once would fire torpedoes from all sides.

Mike's father was on one of those ships.

They went down. Can you imagine what it was like with the explosions and fire and the thought that you are going to die but first you have to get into a lifeboat. Where is that boat?

Murray said Mike told him his father "was being thrown up and down. They watched their ship swallowed by the ocean, nose first."

A monster was eating a morsel.

Look up the war in the Atlantic. Look at the pictures of the ships being hit by U-boats then sinking. Then close your eyes because you cannot watch any more. War is not good.

"They were lost," said Murray repeating what his friend Mike has told him, which Mike had been told by his father.

"It didn't matter which way they went, didn't matter they were still alive, there was no way they would live."

They were in a small lifeboat. They were in the middle of an ocean. Even low swells pushed them to the edges. They had no food, no water, no idea where they were or where they could go because there was nowhere they could go. Instead of dying quickly, they would die slowly.

"Then," Mike said his father told him, "the surface of the ocean started swelling and heaving. They were terrified."

Of course they were. You have probably seen pictures of people fishing in a small boat and suddenly the ocean opens and the back of a whale emerges. Terrifying.

But it was not a whale, it was a submarine that came up next to them.

Imagine. You know a submarine has just shot a torpedo that sunk your ship. The back of the sub rises almost within spitting distance, but your mouth is dry, and your heart is pounding and you know this is the end.

Sailors, German sailors, come out on deck and point a machine gun at you. You get ready to die.

Someone else comes up through the tower and climbs down a ladder. He is obviously the commander because he has no weapons, only authority.

He orders his men to give you food, water and a compass. Then in English he tells you your position.

He climbs back inside. The sailors follow. The sub slides away and slips into the ocean, going after another ship.

"If it wasn't for that," said Murray, "I would not have a friend named Mike."

Yes, of course. Strange, of course. True, of course. Makes you stop and think, of course. Makes you wonder. Makes you shake your head.

After the war Mike's father tried to find Commander Otto Schultz. He got the name after remembering the number of the U-boat.

He wanted to thank him.

Otto Schultz was killed in his ship, as were three-quarters of all German submariners. It was a miserable life, cramped beyond human tolerance, with putrid, unbreathable air from human sources mixed with diesel fumes.

When the submarines dove the sailors had to run to the bow to weigh it down. When it rose, they squeezed into the aft to lift the bow. They were human ballast.

War is not good.

But Murray has his friend in Saint John, and the city workers in Vancouver cleaned the monument, which in a few days would be surrounded by many of those who have never seen, but have read about, the bad times.

And they would say, "War is not good." Murray knew this already, and so did his friend Mike.

A Side Note

This does not belong with this story, but it reminded me of something in a strange way.

When my mother died of lung cancer I got to her side after the doctors told me she was brain-dead.

A machine was breathing for her. That was terrible. The machine took a breath then exhaled through a tube into my mother's destroyed lungs which made her near-dead body breathe.

I kneeled by the side of her bed.

The machine exhaled and her chest swelled, then collapsed. This was not life.

I told her I loved her. A tear came from the side of the eye closest to me. I don't think she had ever cried before this in her life.

We gave permission, no, actually, we requested that her machine be unplugged.

After she died we found some old pictures of her. In almost all of them she was smoking. Everyone smoked back then. It was the war. It was the peace. It doesn't matter what the excuse, everyone smoked.

She smiled and had a cigarette. She posed with friends and had a cigarette.

While she worked as a typist she had a cigarette. Everyone had a cigarette.

We left the hospital and a bus passed by. It had a full-sized ad on the side: "You've come a long way, baby," it said, with a picture of a beautiful woman, smoking a cigarette.

There was a famous anti-war song during the war in Vietnam that asked if we would ever learn enough to stop killing each other.

The question applies to shooting, hating, even smoking. The song asked the question, but there was no answer.

A Trigger in Every Finger

A Little Suggestion to America About Its Gun Problem

S tart with the basics: If you are over sixteen you must carry a gun.

What sixteen-year-old wants to be face to face with another sixteen-year-old, arguing about that girl over there, and not be armed?

If both of you have a gun, it makes the argument fair and square. You both can shoot, and she can find someone she actually likes.

But just one gun is not enough.

Suppose you drop your gun, or as in the old western movies, someone shoots it out of your hand? What then?

That requires an amendment to the us Second Amendment.

The solution? Simple: Everyone over the age of sixteen would be required by law to carry two guns. One pistol in a holster neatly tucked under your arm giving you that undercover look of authority. And the other a rapid-fire rifle, preferably an AR-100 (Who cares about an AR-15? We are looking for real power), which you will sling over your shoulder.

That way everyone will know you can defend yourself if some nutcase starts attacking you or threatening nearby women and children.

The National Rifle Association says you never know when something like that will happen.

Women, especially mothers, would also be required to carry a handgun, in pocket or purse, and a semi-automatic rifle on the back of their baby carriage in the event that the previously mentioned nutcase attacks them and no one is around to help out.

It might also help, though it would not be required, for a mother to carry a second semi-automatic rifle near her diaper bag under the carriage.

Suppose, just suppose, the baby knocked the first semi onto the ground while she was reaching for her stuffy and the mother did not notice?

What then?

Those who oppose gun control would be the first to be required to carry at least two guns. There would be checks as they enter and leave work or church.

That would be the law. No arguments. Remember, those in charge have the guns.

But no child under sixteen will be allowed to be armed, without the supervision of an adult.

We do not want to influence them while they are still growing.

In the end, there will be no denouncing the National Rifle Association because everyone will automatically be a member. No complaints from the anti-gun people because there won't be any.

And no one telling the news media they are shocked because someone who was known for being friendly and quiet and unarmed suddenly went on a shooting rampage, because everyone who is friendly and quiet will be armed. Plus his neighbours will be ready for him.

As for those ghastly news reports of "Yet another shooting," there will not be any. Gun smoke in the air will be like a fender bender on the street.

Too common to report on.

Problem solved.

John L. Sullivan

Hard Way to Become Rich and Famous

L ike you, I don't like violence.

Okay, some of you may. But just a little, and only in the movies.

But I have a double standard, like many. I say I don't like something but sometimes I do.

Life is how you see it.

When I learned that John L. Sullivan had been in Vancouver numerous times, I was thrilled. I told a couple of friends, older ones, all men, and they also were excited.

I mentioned it to some younger people.

"Who?"

"John L. Sullivan," I said with the tone that says without saying it, "How could you *not* know?"

John L. Sullivan was the last bare-knuckle boxing champion in the world. There! You must now be impressed. Except now there is an attempt to start up bare-knuckle boxing again. Is nothing sacred?

"Yuck," you say, if you hate any kind of violence, even in the past, and have never seen a war movie or a gladiator movie or a movie about dinosaurs or sharks or UFOs invading the earth. I admire your commitment.

But if you have a double standard like me, you say secretly about John L. Sullivan, "Wow," because, well, because that is something you could have been in your secret dreams. The very secret ones. You could have been a bare-knuckle boxer.

To explain it to those who are still saying, "Who?"

John L. Sullivan stood in a boxing ring with his fists uncovered and pounded his knuckles into another man, also with his fists uncovered, until one of them fell down.

They did not dance around like modern fighters. They just hit each other.

"Yuck," you say again, especially if you have sensitivity and kindness in your heart and are a vegan.

Let us get down to the hard facts of bare-knuckle boxing.

No one in this contest ever said, "I quit."

In many fights both men got so bloodied that the fans could not tell them apart.

There was one fight where both John L. and his opponent could no longer lift their arms. That was after seventy-five rounds. The referee called it a draw. The fans booed.

They had their bets down and now, "What? Who won? What about the time I've put in watching them, and I get nothing out of it? A couple of fakes."

Human kindness has room to evolve.

In the late 1800s bare-knuckle boxing was the biggest sport in the world. A few baseball catchers behind the plate were starting to wear thin leather gloves, wimps, and leather helmets were starting to show up on football fields—again, wimps.

But in the ring, it was uncovered fist against uncovered fist. This was a sport few men would go into though most men said if they were in there they would have been great. Always the double standard.

When I was a copy boy at a newspaper in New York I went out with photographers and reporters almost every night covering crimes and fires and disasters and the other stories of human failings and heroism.

One place I often went was Madison Square Garden when there were boxing matches. I would get under the ring, under the tight hard canvas floor on which two men were punching each other into oblivion.

The photographer I was with would lean up against the edge of the ring to get pictures. When he finished a roll of film he would hand it to me and I would run back to the newspaper.

But while I was under there I heard the squeaking of the boxers' shoes coming down on my head followed by the *umph*s and *ugh*s. I heard the leather-covered fists smashing into jaws and then a pause in the squeaking. I knew someone was stunned.

I did not know then that his brain had probably smashed into the back of his skull and would never work right again. I learned that forty years later when football people figured it out and I said, "Oh, those poor boxers." No wonder they were babbling idiots after they got out of the ring.

But still it was a good education. I learned some people love to see other people hurt other people. From under the ring I watched people in the front row who were watching the fighters.

The pair of spectators I most remember was a very large—okay, fat—man, his vest and jacket stretched over his large girth and a cigar in his mouth, and a blonde woman with a fur wrap around her shoulders and a strings of pearls around her neck. She was screaming, "Kill him! Kill him!"

Of all the fights I have seen, that woman in the front row is my sharpest memory. It was not the hurting above me that was bad, but the wanting for someone to get hurt. I think that causes more hurt than even those who are doing the hurting.

It taught me to be careful of those who call for war but don't have a uniform.

On the other hand, that was John L. Sullivan's world, long before boxers put on gloves. He did the hitting in the most brutal manner and he got hit the same way and surrounding him were hundreds of people all screaming at him to hurt someone else, or someone else to hurt him.

Tough job.

Then he retired and visited Vancouver. And that, of course, is what this is about.

He gave up boxing and took up acting. And he was a bad actor. But even though he forgot his lines, they had to turn away crowds every night. They came to hear him forget. Yes, you don't have to be good to be a big draw.

And why could he not remember the lines he was supposed to say? In his former job he wasn't paid for his brains and in that job his brain had been bounced around for years. But he was John L. Sullivan and he was a hero in the biggest sport of the late 1800s.

He was kind, he was gentle, he was funny, he promised to try not to drink too much before he went on the stage so that he could try not to say anything that would embarrass the audience who was hoping he would forget his promise and embarrass himself or them.

He performed at the Pantages Theatre. He came here numerous times. There is no record of why he liked Vancouver. It was far from his world in Boston, but he came.

And what makes it wonderful that he was here? The fact that he was here, and he was John L. Sullivan. What more do you want?

John L. Sullivan came and tried to be an actor. It is almost like saying he came to my house and had a beer, or a six-pack before there were six-packs, and we talked all night long. Same meaningless thing, except it was him.

What he did was give Vancouver bragging rights.

And what did he regret? That he did not invest more in real estate. In 1892 he bought a little land in Point Grey. But that was all. Ten years later he said he knew this sleepy cow town would become a great city some day and he wished he had put more money into its land.

What did he do? He saw the future.

And why do I like him? Because he was the last bare-knuckle boxing champion from the true age of bare knuckles. And he came here. And even if I hate violence and cannot stand to watch boxing or Ultimate Fighting and I don't even like fighting in hockey, he was John L. Sullivan.

And he came to Vancouver. Wow. Pretend you are impressed.

Cool Stuff About Hockey

Good Spice Can Melt the Ice

After the Sedin brothers retired I was looking for a related hockey story, something that would hold your interest on hockey, but be different.

Old Canucks players. Not old when they played, but who played long, long ago, before the Canucks joined the National Hockey League. They were then in the Western Hockey League, still tough, hard-core hockey, but not the NHL.

There were dozens of characters. Here are three: Emile Francis, Andy Bathgate and Gump Worsley.

What they give to sports is more than winning or losing. It is more than playing well, which is what you have to do to win. It is a moment, a character, a personality that gives the game spice like biting into a pepper steak.

It is chewy and substantial, but what makes you say "Wow" is the pepper, the best part of a meal or a life. And no, please don't say, "But I don't eat pepper." Please don't.

No excuse. Spice can be mild, like cumin or cinnamon. Spice has flavour. So long as it perks up a meal or a day it is "Wow." It is like something you add to life, something you do—mild, hot, "Wow."

Emile Francis was a goalie. He was spice. He was young. He played baseball. He played first base. He was fast. He was called "The Cat."

He played hockey. He was a goalie because he was fast, but he played with a traditional goal mitt. It was round.

The Cat got to thinking. First base is like being a goalie. You have to stay in one spot and you have to snag anything that comes at you, even if it is not coming directly at you. Darn those wide throws.

Long ago first base players in baseball developed a glove that was like a Venus flytrap: long and flexible, and best of all, it snapped shut. You cannot play first base and drop a ball.

He brought his baseball mitt to the ice rink. Of course, it took some modifications and additional padding, pucks have sharp edges, but then he could snag shots that were otherwise impossible.

One small bright idea made a major change thanks to one hockey player who played baseball.

And Andy Bathgate, one of the best players ever. The fascinating thing about him is he fought against violence on the ice. The early 1960s was a time of war in the rinks. The stick was the main weapon and spearing the form of attack.

If you drove the point of the hockey stick blade into someone's lower back, you could rupture their spleen or smash their kidneys. Besides the look of agony when they turned around, what more could you hope for? It was easier than fighting face to face.

Bathgate, with the help of a professional sports reporter, wrote an article that appeared in a major national us magazine. Bathgate said this violence had to stop before someone was killed.

He named those he thought were the worst offenders.

In answer the league did the only thing it could when it was presented with a common-sense criticism: it fined him one thousand dollars. That was when he was earning just eighteen thousand dollars a year.

Ironically, what Bathgate is most remembered for is an act of brutality. After he was speared by goalie Jacques Plante as he was going by the net, Bathgate said he would teach Plante a lesson.

Most good hockey players can shoot the puck with the same bull's-eye accuracy as major league baseball pitchers.

Bathgate got the puck not too far, not too close to the net and shot it at the face of Plante.

It hit his right cheek and nose.

Plante left the ice and a doctor took a needle and thread and stitched up the gash. Eighteen stitches. Hockey players are tough. The rest of us would have spent the night in the emergency room, then a week at home groaning about the pain and collecting get-well cards.

Plante was back on in the next period, but with something new: a mask. He put it over his bloody face and became the first goalie to wear it in every game.

He learned a lesson, but not the one Bathgate wanted to teach him. He did not learn to put a stop to violence, but he learned to build up his defences.

Such a human trait. You have missiles? We have more missiles!

But we are talking hockey.

Finally, my favourite guy, Gump Worsley. His real name was Lorne John Worsley, but he had a funny face, sort of like a cartoon character named Gump. The cartoon is no longer published. It would be incorrect now to make fun of someone's looks.

Not then, in the distant past, when everything was different. Gump was rookie of the year in 1952 with the New York Rangers. He was very good, but not smart.

He had the audacity—that means outlandish dumbness and out-of-placeness (okay, that's not a word but it means really, really out of place)—to ask for a five-hundred-dollar-a-year, yes a year, raise. That was after he won rookie of the year.

The team owners would teach him a lesson, along with anyone else who thought they were too good for their small salaries. They demoted Worsley to the minors.

He went on to be a goalie, with no mask, in four Stanley Cup–winning seasons.

Only one thought: Can you imagine any player in any professional sport now surviving what they did, even with a mask and a five-hundred-dollar-a-year raise?

The Poor, Poor Bentley

If You Are Rich You Still Should Learn the Basics

I t was backing down the street, on Lonsdale in North Vancouver.
It's a busy street. The Bentley had passed a parking space, so it was coming back, but not back a car length or two. It was speeding back more than half a block against traffic. Backwards. On Lonsdale. In a Bentley. With cars coming up, it was going back down.

Again, a Bentley. Two hundred thousand dollars.

It got to the space and tried to back in.

Missed.

Pulled out and tried again. Missed, again.

Then zoom-zoomed off like a race car, with a foot to the floor on the gas pedal, which to the Bentley must have felt like a tight shoe on a corn on a sore toe.

It is not easy to feel sorry for a piece of machinery. But I did. Poor car.

This Car Is Made for Drivers

Advertising Is Hitting the Right Note No Matter How Wrong It Is

Volvos are made for drivers. That sounds dramatic.
I'm a driver. I need a Volvo.
Wait a minute. I drive a Honda.
Honda has not told me their cars are made for drivers.
And I know someone with a BMW. Their ad said it was a mountain killer.
I don't want to kill a mountain.
But the ad did not say it was made for drivers.
And I saw a Rolls-Royce in West Point Grey.
Of course.
But the slender guy who got out of the car
looked like a real estate agent.
Not a driver.
I think a driver is someone who hears the ads and says, "I believe them.
I can drive better than anyone. I'm a driver."
Then he adds, "I'll get a Volvo. No! Not a Volvo! Never a Volvo.
Volvos are for families. For people to keep their kids safe. I don't
   have kids."
They said that a few years ago when they said Volvos were the safest car.
   Now Volvos sell cars for drivers. But according to Mazda, drivers
   want zoom zoom.
It is hard to keep up with the advertising.
If I want speed I should have a Lamborghini, or a Maserati. Those are
   cars made for drivers who go zoom-zoom, drivers on Robson Street
   who go one hundred kilometres per hour for ten metres.
Then stop. Quickly.

I saw a mother dropping off her child at a daycare in West Point Grey
and she was driving a Maserati.
Can a mother dropping off her kid in a Maserati be a driver?
Of course, a zoom-zoom driver would say, "Mothers going to daycares
are not drivers. They are mothers, going to daycare, who drive."
It seems silly she has a Maserati when she goes zoom-zoom away from
the daycare.
Cars are silly and pretentious and ridiculously fast and expensive to
repair and they get old and go out of style so quickly.
I don't need a driving course,
I need a course in understanding drivers.

The Pickup

He did not have a Ferrari.

He wore a hard hat. He pushed a wheelbarrow.

He lifted two-by-fours. He worked in the rain.

He drove a pickup. He loved his pickup.

It is Canada's best-selling vehicle.

This is a hard-working country.

But, zoom-zoom. A Ferrari zoomed past the site he was working at.

Zoom.

Let's say that better:

Zooooooom!

Better, more honestly:

ZooooooooooooooooooooM!

Followed by:

zoooooom!

With the muffler that cost more than he made in a week.

It hurt his ears.

He got into his pickup. Big steering wheel. Big dashboard. Big windshield.

Made for work.

He stomped on the gas. The exhaust was blue.

Red and blue lights behind him. Flashing.

He said a bad word and pulled over.

"Why'd you do that?" asked the cop.

"Stupid," he said.

"Yes," said the cop.

"Don't do it again," said the cop.

"You mean I can go?" he said.

"Don't be like those idiots," he said.

And the pickup drove home, like a hard-working truck.
And not like an idiot.
Ever again.

Left Side of the Road

No Matter What You Expect, Expect Something Else

J anuary 1, 1922, changed everything.

There would be disaster. Every hour, ten would die.

Roads would be impassible. Children would forget left from right.

And worst of all, truly worst, we would no longer be *British*!

That was the problem with switching from driving on the left side to driving on the right side of the road. It was not a Canadian problem, because every other city and town in the country, including Victoria, which was more British than the British according to a fine book about the city, was already driving on the right.

But *not* Vancouver. Here they were British, or at least that was their fantasy, and their argument for staying on the left.

They cooked dinner by boiling meat, sang "God Save The King" and drove on the left.

A household dinner conversation in Vancouver in December 1921:

"My dear, if we drive on the other side of the road we will be capitulating to those Americans."

"But, my dear husband, there are many advantages to driving on the right."

"Name one that does not make us less British."

"We could go to Blaine for petrol."

"Money does not matter," said the husband. "Being British is an acceptable expense."

But, added the wife:

"Some day when our children's children's children go to Bellingham to shop at Costco they will not cause confusion in the parking lot."

"They can just stay here and pay more for milk, and like it," said the husband.

"And when our descendants try to smuggle wine back across the border they will have to hide it on the right side of the car so the border guard will not see it when he looks in and asks if we have any wine," said the wife.

"They can buy Canadian wine, which by that time won't be bad but will cost twice as much," said the husband.

"And when they go to Disneyland they may put our great-grandchildren into one of their wax figure exhibits of oddball people," said the wife.

"We will vacation in Point Roberts which will then have more Canadians than Americans and there is no place to drive to once you are there."

But regardless of the arguments, at six o'clock in the morning on January 1, 1922, traffic and streetcars switched. There were no accidents. No complaints. No problems. The switch from British driving to American driving happened in a very Canadian way.

A major part of Blaine's economy now comes from Canadian drivers filling up after pulling in from the right-hand side of the road. Costco is crowded with Canadians, and somehow American wine makes it across the border.

"God Save the King," or Queen, is no longer sung in schools and meat is no longer boiled.

Blame it all on January 1, 1922.

Getting Even

Some Things Don't Matter if They Are True

She pulled her gleaming black Mercedes suv into the disabled parking spot in front of the liquor store at the mall. She had a permit with a picture of a wheelchair on it hanging behind her windshield.

She got out. She had lightly curled hair from a beauty parlour. You know the look. Pocketbook over her shoulder.

No cane. No walker. No wheelchair. She went into the liquor store.

Annabelle Grant watched. Annabelle is my friend and she is tough, very tough. And she is fearless. And she does not wait for others to fix things. She fixes them.

She was sitting in an electric wheelchair. She has been in a wheelchair all her life. She did not have to ask how a person who can walk parked in a space for persons who cannot walk. She knows that you cannot see some disabilities. But she has studied this every day of her life and knows when someone walks like they have no disability and acts like they have none, they probably have none and they do not need that spot. She has seen this many times.

Someone in the driver's family has a problem, which allowed for the permit. This is the permit that is supposed to be used when someone needs a wide parking spot in a convenient place. It is not supposed to be used to make parking convenient for the rest of the family when they don't want to walk a few extra steps.

Annabelle drove her electric wheelchair behind the polished suv. Then she shut off her electronic motor and turned on a worried look.

The woman with the curly hair came out of the liquor store carrying a white plastic bag that said, "Drink Responsibly." It did not say to park responsibly.

"I'm so sorry," said Annabelle. "I'll try to get this started before your companion comes out."

"I don't have a companion," said Curly Hair.

"But you are parked in a disabled spot."

"My mother has trouble walking," said Curly Hair.

"Isn't she with you?" asked Annabelle.

"I told you, I am alone."

"Then why are you parking here?"

"Because I'm allowed to."

Annabelle tilted her head and had a perplexed look, the kind you have when someone says two plus two is not strictly what you have always believed two plus two is, and it can be any number they say it is.

"No, you're not."

"Yes, I am."

This is the two plus two argument. Two plus two equals anything you want it to be when you are wrong.

"You can only park here when you have a disabled person in the car," said Annabelle.

"No, I can park here any time I want. I have the permit. And I'm in a hurry to get back."

In front of the suv was a concrete block. Behind it was an electric wheelchair.

"I'm afraid I'm stuck. If you call the manager of the store I'm sure they can help," said Annabelle.

"I can't do that," said Curly Hair.

"Why not?"

"Can't you get that thing moving?" said Curly Hair.

"Oh, I'm afraid I can't. You see, I'm disabled," said Annabelle.

"This is ridiculous," said Curly Hair. "Are you sure that thing won't start?"

"Do you want to try?" asked Annabelle.

"I don't know how to operate that," said Curly Hair.

"I didn't think so," said Annabelle.

Curly Hair was now angry. "What does that mean?"

"I think you would really have to be disabled to work this."

Curly Hair opened her door and put her bag inside.

"I have to go," she said.

"I can't go," said Annabelle. "Please go inside and get some help."

"No."

Annabelle turned her key, the wrong way. Silence. "See, nothing happens. I will call my husband. He can be here in half an hour."

"Can't we just pick this up and move it?" Curly Hair said, trying not to shout.

"Oh, yes. But this is heavy. It would take several strong men. Could you please go and see if you can find them?"

Curly Hair apparently saw this as a way out. She looked around the parking lot and walked off and quickly came back with three young men who looked strong and concerned.

"Can you pick up this wheelchair," she said, pointing to Annabelle, "and let me get out of here?"

"That won't be necessary," said Annabelle.

She turned the key, twisted the handle grip and started to drive away.

Curly Hair shouted at her: "You [bad word]."

"I just wanted someone who is pretending to be disabled to know what it's like to be disabled," Annabelle said to the strong young men.

Then she drove off. But she told me she heard one of the strong young men ask the woman parked in the disabled spot, "Are you disabled?"

And she heard, "*No,* but my mother is."

And then she heard, "Can we help your mother?"

And then she just barely heard, "She's not here."

And then Annabelle went into the mall through the door that had a button to open for people with disabilities. She knew they could see her.

"It was a good day," she told me.

Disabled Permits for All

Solution to People Parking in Places They Should Not Park

E veryone without question gets a special Disabled Parking Permit. So everyone can park close to the liquor store, or the grocery store or movie theatre.

And those who need the spots because of crutches or wheelchairs will have the rest of the parking lot for themselves. No hassle, no frustration.

It will be a lot farther to be pushed, farther with the struggle of moving metal poles before they can move their legs, but think of the entertainment. They can watch the horn honking, yelling battles of able bodies fighting over spots for the disabled. It would be such fun.

Problem solved.

The Buried Cemetery

Dead People Are Nice to Visit

O ne of the stories that received the most comments this year was about the old cemetery in Stanley Park.

Before Vancouver was incorporated as a city in 1886 the one official burial ground was in a wooded area way on the outskirts of town.

It ran along the water of Burrard Inlet, so you could get to it by boat, or go through the woods.

There were some families living at the edge of the forest and there had been many Indigenous people living there for centuries.

But when the city became a city, and the city fathers hoped this land would be someday turned into a park, they closed the cemetery and opened a new one far to the south.

The new one was called Mountain View and it was where Thirty-Seventh Avenue and Fraser Street would be. Far away.

When the land around the old cemetery was finally turned into Stanley Park and someone said there should be a road around it, there was this little problem of the graves in the way.

"Well, let us remove the headstones," said someone, "and get to work paving."

"Over the graves?"

"It's been a while. No one will notice," someone maybe said.

And in truth, time passed and no one remembered. If you drive or walk or bike around the park, as soon as you pass the Nine O'Clock Gun you are gliding over dead people.

When you get up to near the lighthouse at Brockton Point you are back on solid ground.

Neat story.

But one who watched it was Rick Harrison, a retired gardener from the park.

Rick is an amazing guy. He is the one who told me about some old fellow who, with the help of a gardener, shot off his wife's ashes from the Nine O'clock Gun. Another story in another book.

But what was nicest about Rick was once a week for years a little old lady in a wheelchair was brought into the park by her caregiver and Rick would have a flower ready for her.

As soon as he saw her coming he'd cut the fresh bloom and walk a long way to present it.

In the seasons where there were no flowers, Rick would make sure he cultivated something that would bloom in some magical way by keeping it growing alongside a wall that got sun and warmth. He would protect that plant as late as he could so that she would get something to go home with.

Nice guy. Period.

But about the cemetery. He said he often thought about those below the cars and bicycles. That was all, just thought about them. After all, there is nothing else you could do.

Then he told me about a body that he discovered right next to the old cemetery while he was working as a gardener. He told me when and where the murder took place and I replied that I thought I knew that murder.

That was when I was still doing crime stories.

We compared information and it turned out that we were talking about different murders. Then we each talked about a few other bodies we had been around in the park and it got to be a kind of macabre game.

Death is the greatest tragedy of all. And the death of someone you know is the worst of all pains.

But if you don't know the person it can become a study in numbers, then a comparison in details and finally, although it is impossible to believe, it can even become humorous and competitive.

"I saw one that was shot twice."

"Well, I saw one that was shot five times."

Then he told me about a body he found which looked like a gang slaying. In a tree next to the departed the killer had carved something which was probably a warning to others.

The police asked him to cut down the tree to use as evidence.

He said he never found out what happened in that case.

We had talked about flowers and plants before, but it was so neat to get into murder, without suffering the pain of knowing the victims.

Tulips, yes. Bodies, yes. It was a good talk over coffee.

Daffodils

Everything Means Something to Everyone, but the Meanings Are Different

I love daffodils more than any other flower.

First, they are the real flowers of spring. Second ... I'll tell you in a moment.

Snowdrops come when it is still winter. Snowdrops are smart. Yes, they have intelligence. A gardener told me that they grow under bushes so they can survive the snow that always falls unexpectedly in the first days of spring.

Crocuses are next. They come when the snowdrops are tired and suddenly you have crocuses where you had nothing. I met a woman once in Shaughnessy, where the rich people live, and she had a million, maybe more, white crocuses that came up along the city-owned boulevard in front of her home, which was larger than most homeless shelters.

She was nice. She said she asked her gardener to plant some white flowers so she would have something pretty to see when she came home at night.

He dug out the dandelions and filled the holes with crocus bulbs. White ones. The first year she had a few hundred. On the vast expanse of the boulevard this was hardly noticed.

In the second year she had hundreds and hundreds. Crocuses spread. In the third year she had thousands.

I heard about her in the fourth year. She had a blanket of white flowers. Thousands and thousands. She was sweet. The flowers were beautiful. And because I have been doing this for years, decades are nothing. I returned ten years later. It was still white at night.

One neat thing about crocuses is that after they have bloomed it is usually time to cut the grass. They disappear until next year.

But back to daffodils.

Cameraman Gary Barndt told me there were daffodils along Pacific Boulevard. He was right. It was an ocean of yellow. He took pictures and I spoke some words that said the flowers were wonderful.

There were millions of them, one woman said.

Then we went into the middle of the city and found one growing in a pot, which two women said was beautiful. It made them smile. That made me happy.

I spoke nice words about them on television. But daffodils have a deeper meaning to me.

This is hard to write. The most beautiful story I wrote on daffodils came at the most difficult, most heartbreaking time. And that does not come close to describing it.

The nineteen-year-old daughter of a cameraman I often worked with was driving up to Simon Fraser University. Her boyfriend was beside her.

Her name was Christa. Suddenly she blurted out that she had forgotten her camera. She had wanted to take pictures of art projects she and her friends had made.

She pulled over to the side of that long uphill road that goes to the school. She said she had to go back for it.

She made a U-turn. She was nineteen. Nineteen-year-olds can go to college and university, they can vote and they will soon take over the world, but nineteen-year-olds don't often think.

Christa pulled out in front of a car going up the hill.

It hit her broadside. She was killed instantly, so the medical people said. If you have ever fallen or been hit by a car and lived you know that "instantly" takes a long time.

You see the car coming in your peripheral vision. You know what is happening. You think, "Oh no. Why did I do that?" You feel the impact. But you do not feel the pain because of wonderful defences in your body that make you immune to hurt for an instant.

You think of your family and friends. You think of the class or meeting you are not going to attend. You wish you had waited a second longer.

All that happens instantly. And then you hear the collision. And then you go blank.

Her body was covered by a tarp.

Her father, John, had made a career of going to accidents and filming things that are hard to look at. This one time, because God is sometimes good to us, He made sure John was far away when the accident report went out on the police radio.

But he soon heard. And later that night I went to their home and sat with John and his wife and their other two daughters. Their grief was so deep they did not know I was there.

A week later they had a funeral. I wanted to memorialize it. Another cameraman and I were a long distance away from the church. I asked for one shot. Only one of the procession of everyone leaving the church. In the background would be the people, in the foreground I hoped for a single daffodil.

But there were no daffodils nearby.

We did something I usually forbid in all stories. I will not allow a leaf or a piece of litter or anything to be moved for a shot. If people see us changing reality in a small way they could think we change it in larger ways. That is what I tell people who hold and use cameras.

But on this sad day I wanted a daffodil. A single daffodil. It was early spring. There were daffodils everywhere, except in front of the church.

I walked a hundred steps away to a field of yellow flowers. I bent down and picked one. I took it back to the cameraman and stood it up in front of his camera.

"Can you do that?" I asked.

He did.

It was the only time in my life I moved something for the camera.

I wrote words about life and death and autumn and spring as the family and the coffin left the church. The daffodil softened the pain in the background.

When the procession had gone we got up from kneeling on the ground. A woman had been watching us.

"What are you doing?" she asked.

We told her, then I gave her the flower.

A few years later, John the cameraman died of cancer. Many, myself included, thought it was at least partially caused by the stress of losing his daughter.

Five years later, Gary Barndt was taking pictures of a million daffodils along a walkway by the ocean. I was thinking of just one.

Despite other flowers coming before them, they are the real flowers of spring. But remember, things have different meanings to all of us. To me, at least one daffodil is the flower of autumn turning to winter.

The story ended with a close-up of just one daffodil.

Requiem for a Fifteen-Year-Old

When Someone Says You Never Know, Someone Is Right

What you saw if you watched it on TV were red and blue lights smashing onto the wet street. And you saw yellow plastic tape: "POLICE LINE DO NOT CROSS." And you saw people in uniforms and plainclothes cops in blue jeans and wearing guns looking for … What were they looking for? Whatever they could find.

It was a death scene. And they were looking for anything, but mostly bullet fragments. Experts would try to track the path of the smooth pieces of steel that ricocheted off bricks at speeds faster than you could see and went through glass and one, just one, went through the metal door of a car that a fifteen-year-old was riding in, comfortable in the back seat.

A half second more or less and it would have missed the flesh and bone. But that half second was not there. So the bullet—fired by one arrogant, invincible seller of chemicals that make the mind float on clouds at another arrogant, invincible seller of chemicals that some people will pay anything for—went through the car door and hit the fifteen-year-old boy.

He was being driven home by his parents after going out for dinner. How safe, how ordinary.

A fifteen-year-old should not be surrounded by flashing blue and red lights. When you are fifteen and a boy sometimes you see a girl you like very much but you are afraid to tell her because you don't know what will happen.

When you are fifteen you should not be lying under a tarp on a wet street.

When you are fifteen you talk to your friends, mostly boys, about what you want to do when you grow up, because growing up sounds so exciting.

When you are fifteen grown-ups will tell you not to worry about what you will do because you have your whole life in front of you.

When you are fifteen you wonder about when you will start shaving and driving and dating.

When a fifteen-year-old gets into a car with his parents he knows things will go in a predictable way. They will get to where they are going, probably home. He will play some video games, maybe do some homework, not exciting but it is one thing he knows for sure.

And then something happens that the fifteen-year-old has nothing to do with.

Some others, filled with anger and hatred and wanting all the money for themselves and fuelled by bravado and armed with weapons that make them feel even stronger, do something ugly.

They do not know the fifteen-year-old. They have never seen him. In truth, they don't care about him. He is just another car passing by that obstructs their shot.

But because of their self-centered, all-consuming, insane stupidity, and their hatred and their greed and their addiction to showing their strength, the fifteen-year-old will never get to tell that girl he likes her.

We haven't found it yet, but there must be some way to stop people from doing really bad and ugly things. There must be a way that a fifteen-year-old can become sixteen.

Something to Make You Laugh

Crossing the Border to Visit Someone in a Nursing Home

Where are you going?

We're going to a nursing home to visit my mother-in-law.

Do you have any food or alcohol?

No, my mother-in-law has not had a drink for years.

I asked if you have any food or alcohol.

No, we have no food or alcohol.

Why did you say your mother-in-law had not had a drink for years instead of answering the question?

Because she hasn't.

Do you bring her any food?

No.

Do you bring her any alcohol?

I just said we don't have any.

You said she has not had a drink for years.

She hasn't. That's why we do not bring her any alcohol.

Do you have a snack with her?

Yes.

What is in that snack?

A bagel and coffee, sometimes cake, sometimes a muffin.

Are you bringing her a bagel?

No, I said we have no food.

Where do you get the bagel if you don't bring it to her?

We buy it at a coffee shop.

Where is the coffee shop?

Near the nursing home.

Do you give your mother a snack on the way to the shop?
No. Why would we do that?
I asked if you give her a snack. Are you avoiding the question?
No. We don't give her a snack on the way to a snack.
Are you getting cute with me?
No. I am answering the questions.
What was the last question?
I'm sorry. I don't remember.
Are you not paying attention?
Yes, I mean no. I mean I am paying attention.
Do you have any food or alcohol?
No.
Okay, enjoy your day.
Honest to heaven, word for word without exaggeration or addition.

The World Is Always Changing

An Assignment for You

I wrote the following story before today happened. I wrote about how bad the relations between every official arm of everything and the media had become before today.

Then today happened.

We were on Commercial Drive, which has its own culture. I love it. Everyone loves it, except for those who are afraid of it.

We passed a fire truck parked on Commercial near Third Avenue. Don't worry if you don't know where that is.

It has Italian restaurants and coffee shops like most of the street. And there on top of the truck we could see firefighters eating lunch and drinking coffee.

"It's a patio lunch," said cameraman Gary Rutherford.

I thought of all that had happened to me in the last half-dozen years regarding relations with the fire department and police and Park Board and said, "So what? They would have to get permission from the office in the sky before they would talk to us, and then the officials in the office in the sky would ask, 'What is your purpose in talking to the firefighters? What is your agenda? What will be your questions?' And they would have to have a person from their media relations office there to monitor our questions and the answers of the firefighters. And they could arrange a meeting of the truck crew and us and the media relations people next week."

None of that is exaggeration.

So I said to Gary, "Are you out of your mind? There is no way they are going to let us see them eating lunch on top of their truck. No way at all."

Then I added, "I'll get out and ask, but don't count on it."

I got out. He looked for parking. I looked up at the firefighters eating on the roof of their truck.

"Excuse me, none of our business," etc., you have read this before, "but can we take a picture of you eating up there and put it on television?"

No sense hiding the obvious.

"Sure," says the big man in charge. I could tell he ran the ship, or the truck, because he was older and larger, which young firefighters are not. The young ones are trim and get in calendars and hope to save lives.

The older ones don't get in calendars and have already saved lives.

We climbed up on the top of the firetruck. There were a handful of firefighters in blue uniforms with meatball sandwiches and salami sandwiches and, well, come on, what else would you order on Commercial Drive? If you are a vegetarian go to West Fourth.

And they were gracious and showed us around their truck, which they said was the finest in North America. These firefighters were members of the department's technical rescue team. They save people. Their truck had everything you would need to grab someone who was caught in a river or stuck on the side of a building that was collapsing, which seldom happens, but boy, you would be thankful if it did and you were there and these saviours showed up.

The truck had endless pieces of equipment, from two-by-fours to metal things that they know how to work but no one else would. You get the idea.

Actually, you might not. There is a universe that is often lost in the words that try to describe it. There is nothing I have said that connects you to the idea that these were people who save lives by risking their own.

There was a time when readers of newspapers in their homes or going to work on subway trains could almost feel what it was like to watch these people work. And that was because we were allowed to report on it. It was a different age.

During that time, I was in New York. And I was at a tenement building, which means a building for poor folks, and a kid, maybe seven or eight, had somehow gotten his leg caught between an elevator and the edge of the landing.

The pain was worse than unbearable. What does that mean? He screamed until he could scream no more.

Here is where I will jump ahead with you to where the police emergency response team came, and I was there because I was allowed to be there.

Traffic in New York was bad. Drivers hardly pulled over for a fire truck. "Like, get real. Where are we going to pull over to?" No one pulled over for a police car. "They will just have to wait, like the rest of us."

But for the Emergency Service Unit, New Yorkers got out of the way. The firefighters we met on top of the truck in Vancouver do the same work as that police unit of long ago.

In New York they drove boxy cars that everyone recognized. Those inside carried pistols only because they were required to. What they mostly had in their pockets were wrenches and pliers, and instead of handcuffs hanging from their belts they had wire cutters and duct tape.

What you saw when they got to a scene was rope coiled over their shoulders and crowbars in their hands.

They saved people.

They went under the subway cars and saved those caught under them. Those under cars and hanging from the sides of buildings, no matter how they got there, were brought down, and those with a leg caught between an elevator and the floor were rescued.

There was no telling how long the boy was there. No telling how long he screamed or how long before someone called 9-1-1.

I was there just after the first police. The kid was in agony. The kid was terrified. I was terrified for the kid.

The Emergency Service Unit was there minutes later.

When I began this job the world was different. There were no restrictions on reporters. They were treated as a way to let the public know what was happening.

I did a lot of crime stories and unless I was going to step on some evidence no one stopped me from looking into the eyes of the departed Mafia hoodlum who had recently gained several holes in his suit, which he was still wearing.

I had a press card that said I could pass all police and fire lines. In small print it added that I would take responsibility and afford no blame to anyone else if I should acquire similar holes in my jacket.

It was the same in Vancouver as New York, minus the Mafia.

When a young girl was abducted and held for six months in a bomb shelter ten feet below a garage and was found only by the will of God, I was there shortly after she was taken out.

The police said there was no problem with me going down the ladder in the shaft that stopped at the padded door behind which she was locked. There was no hesitation about me going into the tiny room where she was held. No problem with me seeing the handcuffs still on the bed. No problem with me turning around and closing the door and feeling alone and terrified.

I at least had a small idea of what she went through. I wrote about this numerous times. I talked about it on television. I talked about it in speeches.

My reporting did not affect the trial. The accused pleaded guilty and was sentenced to many, many years in prison. He died there.

The last time I saw the young girl she had somehow not only survived but was happy, with two daughters of her own.

Because I saw it I was able to let others know how terrible it was for her. They felt it, at least as best as I could describe it. If I had not done that, very simply, no one would know the pain, the faith, the strength, the unbelievable, and I mean unbelievable, will of a girl who turned thirteen imprisoned underground and was repeatedly raped and tortured for six months.

Because the man pleaded guilty there was no testimony in court. And therefore there was no reporting in newspapers or television.

That was a long time ago. Now we would get a press release that would say she was found through police investigation and that the accused was in custody. Period. No stifling air, no claustrophobia, no terror, no tears.

Now every crime scene is off limits. Even after the crime. There are many reasons. Some good, some not. But every crime is now seen through a press release, given by one friendly police officer who is very good at handling the media.

It is nice that he or she does that. But we have only one view of what happened.

I am not blaming or condemning the police. I give this only as an example because everything is now controlled in its output.

There was a time when I walked into a fire station and was told about a woman who baked cookies for the firefighters. And I was told she would be there in a few minutes, and she was.

They were her boys. She opened the cookies and the bell rang. The firefighters left. She sat at a table in the empty station and waited. It was a beautiful story.

There was another time I was in Burkeville. Pretend you know this place because it has been in several books and many television stories. It is even in this book, in a story about clotheslines. Burkeville is at the end of the runway at the airport.

There are no stores in Burkeville, no place for kids to get candy, but also no crime, no sidewalks, no drive-by shootings, nothing but ditches along the walkways where kids can fish for tadpoles.

Not a bad life, but again, no candy.

I passed by one day and asked why so many kids were going in and out of the back of the fire station right at the edge of Burkeville.

"We have a candy store inside," said a firefighter. "Come and look."

I did and by golly, that is what they had. They had candy and pop and chips and the firefighters sold them at face value. That saved the kids from crossing an extremely busy and dangerous street to get to a real corner store.

The story was happy, about kids getting to know the heroes of the community and feeling comfortable with them.

Ten years later, at the same fire station I asked a firefighter standing outside what was new.

"I can't talk to you without permission," he said.

"You're kidding."

"No."

Now, no one, at least not people like me, can find out the wonderful things going on inside a place filled with firefighters without prior permission given by the media relations department downtown.

And there is no permission given for just casually running into stories about sweet ladies with cookies or kind firefighters with candy.

I know this sounds bitter, but it is not me that is hurting as much as you.

This control extends to gardeners at the city parks. No more can I ask about tulips or dandelions without permission, and no gardener is allowed to speak to me without permission.

I have been told I can always get it because the powers that be know me, but how would anyone get permission ahead of time just to casually ask about an obscure clump of beautiful flowers that you did not know were there?

So no more stories with expert advice about clumps of beautiful flowers. I still put the flowers on the air, but they do not come with advice from gardeners.

Sorry I keep going on, but I have been part of this industry for more than half a century and this has been the worst thing that has happened to it.

It is so bad that lifeguards on the beaches are not allowed to talk to the media about the weather without prior approval.

And the worst areas of this control are the community centres. They are the heart of human interaction, imagination, sometimes love and often barefoot Ping-Pong games. Especially on rainy days.

Until a few years ago, I could go into a community centre, talk to the person in charge and ask if anything wonderful or strange was happening. And that someone would often direct me to a card game that had not had a definite winner in five years, or a kid learning to play the violin on her own time without being ordered to.

I would get permission from the parent or the people involved, and make sure no one who did not want to be on television was filmed and do stories that were a delight to watch.

Now I am not allowed in without permission ahead of time and that of course is impossible to get if I do not know what is inside.

And this is why virtually all my stories have moved outside where organizations and governments have no control. Outside, on sidewalks, in parks (so long as we don't talk to gardeners), on beaches (so long as we don't talk to lifeguards), in back alleys and in front yards where we the people live—that is where these stories have come from over the past decade. Outside is perfect because that is where *you* are. And I am always looking for you when you are planting a garden or walking around a tree.

But this is also an opportunity for you.

While institutions have been putting walls around themselves to keep the official media out, they are letting you in.

All the places closed off to the media are open to you. Gardeners are lovely people and most of them would go out of their way to tell you about tulips and dandelions.

The recreation centres are open for exploring as well as exercising. You can find the barefoot Ping-Pong player and think, that's crazy, but it is neat.

And the courts, where the rules make it very difficult for reporters to report, have no restrictions on what you hear or take notes about. You can sit in on a case and marvel at the speed that is not there and listen to lawyers using many words to say few things.

And then you can pray you never have to go to court where someone in a very expensive suit says things that you don't understand, which may or may not save you but will cost you more than you can afford.

It's an education.

If you walk up to a fire hall and talk to whoever has the job of washing the trucks and ask what's new, the scrubbing will stop and the answers will start.

Firefighters are especially nice people. One riding in a big truck waved to me while I was on a bus last week. I honestly felt so good. Thanks, whoever you were.

Back to New York and the boy stuck in the elevator. I watched the emergency workers try to ease the crush of the steel box away from his leg. Then others went down to the floor below and put up ladders that went from one side of the elevator shaft to the other, and then back again.

Below them were six or seven stories of falling, which meant dying. They got on the ladders which were leaning against walls covered with grease and climbed up under the elevator and with hand wrenches started taking apart the elevator.

Can you imagine that? It would be hard to do if it was sitting on a concrete floor. But they were using hand-held wrenches to undo the bolts that were holding the big box that was above their heads.

And they were doing it slowly and carefully and at the same time quickly and carefully so that they would not let the box move toward the boy's leg. And below them was a hole of blackness that if they slipped would kill them.

That is why the cars in the thick of traffic in New York got out of the way of the Emergency Service Unit.

It is easy to say they freed the boy. But it is not easy to say how the minutes were terrifying and how a doctor talked calmly to him and gave him a shot to deaden the pain.

In short, the emergency unit moved the elevator enough to get the boy's leg free. He was rushed to a hospital and I was at the door of the room when inside another doctor stuck a needle into the boy's foot and when the boy yelled the doctor told his mother that his leg would be saved.

In a minute I was on a pay phone to a rewrite person in the newsroom of the newspaper I worked for. And in an hour the story was on the street being read by people who learned how brave were those who saved the boy, and how brave was the boy. The readers were there, while he was saved.

If it happened now, we would get a press release the next day.

This is your assignment: If you like, you can change the world. You have your social media to do your own stories. Write them, take pictures, share them. You are allowed to go almost anywhere. You will have my job and my life, and you may find it is pretty good. You don't need a television station to do it, and if you do it well enough you may get paid for it. Don't ask me how—I don't understand the new world of social media.

And of course, stay away from bad stories. That is, unless you like crime and disasters. Go watch a fire or an accident or a routine police procedure.

It was someone recording a poor fellow getting struck repeatedly by tasers at the airport that ensured that people leaving flights can no longer get trapped in an area where they cannot see out and no one can see in.

It was not a member of the media who took those pictures.

But mostly what I think you should do is go out and do what I do, and have fun.

And no one will tell you to get permission ahead of time.

And that was what I had been complaining about.

But then today happened, May 7, 2018, and the firefighter up on the truck on Commercial Drive said, sure, we could climb up and see their mobile patio.

I was stunned.

It was a fun story, a nice story about people who do exactly the same thing as I saw in the elevator shaft in New York. The only difference is in Vancouver the fire department has special units that save us when we are going to kill ourselves by jumping off a bridge, or when we get stuck upside down in a pipe we were looking down into.

The story was simply about them having lunch while sitting on the top of their truck which gave them a personal patio on Commercial Drive.

We have lunch at a desk. They have it on their truck. That was all. I loved it. It was like the old days, except this had no pain and suffering.

I half expected a phone call later from some official downtown who would say that because we did not get official permission we could not use the story, the reason being we did not get official permission.

The phone call never came.

And after lunch the truck and its crew went off to be trained in how to hang by ropes under a bridge to save lives. Pretty impressive.

And I no longer have anything to complain about.

Some Warmth

What Good Could Come from a Fire?

T he blaze broke out in apartment 317. It was caused by a faulty electrical socket.

Smoke alarms went off, then the bells rang throughout the building. Seven stories high, ten apartments on each floor in the front, and ten in the back that had the best views of the mountains.

It started at seven thirty, a little later than the usual alarms which came at dinner time. Alarms went off when a pot was burning on the stove. They went off every couple of days.

Marty, on the top floor, paid no attention.

Gus, on the third floor, said it was the biggest fire they'd ever had.

Evelyn, on the seventh floor, said she hoped nothing bad was happening because this was the best place she had ever lived in.

The fire wasn't bad, not too bad. The firefighters came and they broke into apartment 317 and carried a woman out in her wheelchair. They carried her down the stairs and to the ambulance, which took her to St. Paul's Hospital, and although she was in serious condition she would be okay.

"Serious condition" is the technical term for sort of in the middle, between "Oh, my god," and "Don't worry, it's not so bad."

The next morning we were out in front of the building. It is old, thirty or forty years. It is made of concrete, which in its natural colour of light beige does not age well. It looked old, and worn. A torn Canadian flag hung from one window. CDs hung on strings and played in the wind over a balcony. The building is in one of the most expensive neighbourhoods in the city, but looks like an intruder.

255

It is a home for those who need help, but not too much help. It is for coal miners who have trouble breathing. And for alcoholics who are not drinking. And drug addicts who are clean. And for those who are old and have nothing but government pensions. It is a massive building for those with hard lives.

And it is also a home for those who used no drugs and no alcohol but got old and could not find jobs and their bank account balances went down and their credit card balances went up and there was no help but bankruptcy. It is a home for someone who was an executive secretary in an age that does not use executive secretaries any more.

Fire department investigators went inside. Outside the building we talked to those who were safe but still felt the excitement of the flashing red lights and hoses and trucks and television cameras from the night before.

"It was the biggest fire ever," said Gus, who was in his electric scooter.

Near him was Marty, who was younger than Gus. He was going in the door when we stopped him and asked about the building.

"It is interesting," he said.

We asked, "What do you mean?"

He said, "There are drug addicts and reformed alcoholics and desperate people and old folks here."

Then he said he had been off the drink for six years. I said congratulations. He said thank you.

He earned the praise.

His description of the building is what you say when you are trying to be nice but you don't really mean it.

Everyone in Sunset Towers, a terrible name, on Barclay Street, in the middle of high-cost, high-rent, high-priced, high-trendy West End, is on social assistance.

Many who live there are in a secret fight with demons while many in the surrounding neighbourhood are struggling to surpass last week's style. It is a tough life.

But we are there for the fire.

Most did not know the woman who was taken to the hospital. Most did not know those who lived two doors down unless their schedules were identical and even then they would only say hello.

But Evelyn, who could not find a job, and Marty, who was still drinking water despite the powerful urge to go to the store and get something that looked like water and would make him happy for an hour and ruin the next six years, and Gus, who could not breathe because he worked his life below ground digging out the sides of black tunnels and hoping the tunnels did not collapse, were each happy the fire was confined to one apartment, far from theirs.

Two hundred apartments in the building. Evelyn, Marty and Gus were together outside the front door talking about the fire.

"Did you know each other before?" I asked.

"No."

Then Evelyn said, "But this is big news. We all went through this together."

For the first time they met, they talked, they shared, they were neighbours. They decided it could have been much worse. They decided that there should be more practice fire drills. They decided they would try to find the name of the woman who was hurt.

For the first time they were neighbours in their own neighbourhood.

No other news mattered that day.

You Can Trust Us

Put Your Hand on the Television and I Will Make You Rich

I n the old days of black and white and ten-inch screens, the religious shows, especially in the southern US, would have you put your hand on the television and pray with them.

They did the same thing with the radio for years.

They would beseech the heavenly powers to bring you health and money, because you deserved it, they said.

And then they would ask you to help their ministry to do its work by sending a small contribution, "just as much as you're able to, so that we can continue helping others."

Then you would remove your hand and put some dollar bills in an envelope because you did not have a chequing account and you would send it and feel good.

It worked every time.

Our TVs now have no room to place your hand, and if you did you would get fingerprints on the screen, which might interfere with the electrons.

But beyond that, nothing is different.

Now we put our faith in the commercials:

For your wealth, invest in us.

We care. We truly care.

Not like others. They don't care.

We care.

Your future will be golden. We do what others don't.

We care.

Invest in us because we believe in you. If you invest only one hundred dollars or more a week you will be building for your future.

And then over pictures of happy people, who you would swear are only happy because they invest, you hear very quickly:

This product is not intended to be an offering. That can only be done through a licensed seller, which we are not. Future performance is not guaranteed by past performance which we have altered slightly to appear to have been outstanding. Invest wisely. Investment returns are calculated after broker fees and other costs have been deducted.

Invest in us.

We care.

Not like those others.

And for your health:

This Drug Will Fix You

Tired of feeling bad? Tired of being sad?

We have, on sale now, a drug that will make you glad.

No more sad, no more bad. On sale, for a limited time only.

Operators are standing by.

All this while watching happy, healthy people doing happy, healthy things.

We say again, no more sad, no more bad.

And then in very fast words, almost too fast to hear:

This drug is not approved by the people who do the approving and is not intended to be a substitute for proper medical care or common sense.

The words are behind more pictures of happy people who look happy and healthy because they take this drug. Then the words slow:

On sale now.

No more sad, no more bad.

And then they speed up, even faster.

Beware of side effects: swollen legs, slurred speech, trouble sleeping, constipation, stomach cramps, thoughts of suicide, possible death.

The words come over pictures of more happy people who you would swear are happy because they are taking this miracle pill.

This drug will make you glad.

Get 50 per cent off if you call right now.

You will feel glad.

Offer not available in Canada.

Art Works

The Critic Sometimes Does Not Have the Eye of the Beholder

That pretty picture of flowers you have on your wall, or that beautiful sunset painting you have over your fireplace, where did it come from?

I have one of them. It is wonderful. I could not help buying it when I saw it. And I hung it on the wall. And some have said, "Nice." That's good enough for me.

Then I read in the *South China Morning Post* that in a small corner of that country there is the biggest art-producing region in the world.

It is Dafen Oil Painting Village, located in Dafen, Buji Sub-District, Longgang District, Shenzhen City.

There, in an area four-tenths of a square kilometre—we are talking roughly from Burrard to Granville and then from Georgia to Robson—a route you could walk in twenty minutes including stopping for a grilled cheese sandwich from a food truck, there are eight thousand artists painting, every day, every hour, every minute, masterpieces.

There is nothing wrong with this. I love it. It is not a sweatshop. It is a shop of creative, intensely busy artists. It is a village of oils and colours and canvases and journeyman artists and probably some geniuses who can't get a job being geniuses.

Clamp another canvas on the easel, paint flowers in a vase, no wait, I did that this morning, paint a mountain scene, with snow. Good. Done. Let it dry on its way to the shipping room and then do a mountain scene without snow.

In addition to the artists there are twenty thousand people employed here, all wrapping and shipping and calculating profit and loss and finding buyers.

The artists are painting from memory, or photos, or glances at the last masterpiece they created and moving the flowers to the right of the vase instead of the left. They are also famous for reproducing classic paintings for cheap, both legally and less so.

They are raising or lowering the sunset over a tranquil river or having the sun come up over the Arc de Triomphe or having it set.

It is the only industry in this town. And it is thriving.

Seven out of ten paintings in every collection in every home in Europe and America and Canada came from this community. That is what the article said. Maybe, maybe not, but a lot of them do.

Most of the artists have never seen the Arc de Triomphe. I'm taking a guess there. And many have never seen a snow-capped mountain. I'm guessing again, but I think I'm safe.

But they are good. They are artists. It is my guess, and nothing more, that these jobs came along when they were making no money painting pictures of the river near their home.

It is hard to say no when someone says here's money for doing what you love to do, just sign some scribbled name at the bottom. Your time will come, just not today.

And what do I think when I see my painting? It's beautiful. The flower is just right and the vase is just there to the left, or is it to the right? Doesn't matter that I can't remember. It is good to see when I come home from work.

Do I feel cheated because it was basically turned out in a factory and the artist may have painted three others that day? No. The artist, whoever he or she is or was, was like so many. He or she went to work, punched the time clock, sat at the desk or stood at the easel, but unlike 99 per cent of others who turn out gidgets and gadgets, he or she made something wonderful.

Thank you, whoever you are.

And someday, you may do something in your time off, and someone will recognize it and you will sell a million copies of it.

Until then, I like my original.

You Make Me Feel Good

Yes, you. I have met thousands of you. Maybe more. And mostly, except for the few who are filled with anger, you make me feel good.

You were standing at the bus stop in the rain and let the little old lady on while you stood aside and let the rain fall on you a few moments longer.

You smiled at the person in the wheelchair who had withered legs and barely one arm. You did not look away.

You actually bent over and picked up a part of a newspaper that was on the ground. You did not feel embarrassed. You crumpled it up in your hand and carried it to a garbage can and dropped it in.

You make me feel good.

You are out there doing good things.

I just want to take this moment to thank you.

When things get bad, and they always do, I think about you and I would not change my life or the time in which I am living for anything.

Thank you.

PS

Shoelaces are not so hard after all. Especially when someone helps.